THE USBORNE BOOK OF
KINGS & QUEENS

Philippa Wingate

History consultant: Dr Anne Millard

Designed by Russell Punter

999691
Illustrated by Ross Watton, Peter Dennis,
Simon Roulstone and John Fox

Series editor: Anthony Marks

Contents

Introduction

Amenhotep IV

Hippolyte

Shih Huang Ti

An Oba of Benin

Matilda

Henry VIII

What is a king or queen?

A king or a queen is the single ruler of a country or an independent state. Kings and queens are also known as monarchs, from the Greek for "single ruler".

Monarchs are given many different titles around the world. You will come across examples of many of them in this book, including sultans and sultanas, rajas and ranis, tsars and tsarinas, pharaohs, khans, shahs and incas. Rulers who control lands so vast that they hold power over other monarchs are often given the title emperor or empress. Some kings and queens gain their title only because they are married to a ruling monarch.

Leadership, past and present

Since the earliest times, leaders have emerged among groups of people. At first they were chosen for their popularity, or their skill as warriors or hunters. Some ancient leaders were believed to have special powers that would bring their kingdoms good fortune. Later, in many countries, power was passed between the members of royal families, usually from father to son.

Today, many of the world's monarchies have disappeared. Most countries are ruled by presidents, elected heads of state who are voted into power for limited periods of time. Other countries are governed by dictators, who seize power and rule by military force.

A selection of monarchs are pictured on this page. You can find out more about their lives and actions in the book.

Montezuma

Elizabeth I

Louis XIV

Napoleon Bonaparte

Victoria

Elizabeth II

About this book

This book explores the lives of some of history's outstanding rulers. It examines how they worked and played, and how myths and mysteries grew up around them. It looks at the ceremonies and regalia which set monarchs apart from ordinary people. The people in this book are not arranged in historical order. They have been selected because their lives illustrate certain themes and topics.

Dates

Some of the dates mentioned in this book are from the period before the birth of Christ. These dates are followed by the letters BC, which stand for "Before Christ". Dates in the BC period are counted backwards from the birth of Christ. For example, the period from 1-99BC is called the first century BC. Dates after the birth of Christ have no letters.

If historians are unsure exactly when an event occurred, the date is shown with a "c" in front of it. This stands for *circa*, which is the Latin for "about".

A coronation is the ceremony at which the power and status of leadership is symbolically transferred to a new monarch. After the ceremony, the new ruler is set apart from ordinary people.

Choosing a monarch

When a monarch dies, a successor is immediately named. The rules of succession vary. In many societies, the monarch's eldest son inherits the throne. In some countries, a monarch chooses a successor from among all the adult male members of his family. In some places women are allowed to claim the crown if there are no suitable male heirs. Elsewhere, women are never allowed to rule in their own name.

Crowning a monarch

In most cultures the coronation ceremony includes some kind of religious blessing and the presentation of a crown to the new monarch.

The crowns of the Egyptian pharaohs

Some pharaohs wore a Double Crown to show they ruled Upper and Lower Egypt

The Red Crown of Lower Egypt

The White Crown of Upper Egypt

The queen's crown

Crowning an English monarch

The coronation ceremony of the kings and queens of England is one of the oldest state ceremonies in the world. Parts of it date back to the 8th century.

The pictures show stages of the coronation of Elizabeth II (b.1926), who was crowned Queen of Great Britain and Northern Ireland in 1953.

A selection of some of the surviving crowns from around the world.

(right) The Holy Roman Empire Crown was made for King Otto I of Germany in the 10th century.

(left) The Imperial Crown was made for Catherine the Great of Russia.

(right) This Kiani crown was made in 1789 for the coronation of Fath Ali, the Shah of Iran.

(left) This crown was made for Louis XVIII of France.

(right) The Emperor of Iran's crown was made in 1924 for the coronation of Reza Shah.

Elizabeth II's coronation

The coach was built in 1761 for George III of England.

The coach is pulled by pairs of horses.

1. The procession – The queen arrives at Westminster Abbey in the state coach. She wears a robe of crimson velvet, trimmed with fur and bordered with gold lace and a diamond crown of precious stones.

2. The recognition – The archbishop introduces the queen to the people in the Abbey as the true monarch and they are asked to accept her.

Enthroned

In early Germanic tribes, a new king was lifted up on a shield, supported by his warriors, so that he could be seen and acclaimed by his subjects. Ceremonies like this have now been replaced in many countries by a special chair or stool on which a monarch sits. The throne is usually placed on a mound or platform, so that the monarch is raised above the people.

A selection of famous thrones

This throne, found in the palace of Knossos, Crete, was probably used by the Minoan kings.

The throne of King Tutankhamun of Egypt is gold-plated and inlaid with semi-precious stones.

The Peacock Throne, used by the Shahs of Iran

The Coronation Chair, made in 1301 for Edward I of England.

Anointing the new leader

Today, many European Christian monarchs are anointed with holy oil during their coronation. They believe that this marks them as God's chosen representatives. The tradition was reintroduced by King Pepin of the Franks (c.715-68), who was the first king to be anointed with holy oil since the kings of ancient Israel. He felt he needed a special sign of divine approval for his reign.

This horn holds the oil used to anoint the new ruler of Sweden.

The oil is poured from this spout.

The gold horn is decorated with diamonds and rubies.

Regalia

Different cultures have various objects which are given to new monarchs at their coronation as symbols of their power. They are known as regalia, and include crowns, rods, staffs, sceptres, orbs, rings, spurs and swords.

An African fly-whisk; a ceremonial sword of the ruler of the Akan (Africa); an Egyptian pharaoh's ceremonial crook

Stealing the crown jewels

During the reign of Charles II of England (1630-85), an Irish adventurer named Colonel Blood attempted to steal the crown jewels. Dressed as a clergyman, he visited the Jewel House in the Tower of London (see page 37) with a woman pretending to be his wife.

While looking at the regalia, the woman appeared to be taken ill. She was helped outside, giving Blood an opportunity to befriend the Jewel House keeper.

Blood stealing the crown jewels

One May morning, Blood returned with three men, and asked to see the regalia. The keeper took them into the Jewel House.

Blood beat the keeper over the head, seized the crown, sceptre and orb and, inexplicably, ran toward the farthest exit.

The thieves were stopped by the keeper's son. After a brief fight they were overpowered and arrested.

Blood was not punished. Charles II awarded him a pension and some land. Some people suspected the king had used Blood to steal the jewels, hoping to sell them to raise some much-needed money.

A new dragon king

In the fourth month of the Wood Tiger Year, at the Hour of the Serpent (June 2, 1974), Jigme Singye Wangchuck became King of Bhutan, known to its people as the Land of the Dragon. The coronation cost the country a fifth of its annual budget.

The king placed on his shoulders a shawl that belonged to his great-great grandfather, the first King of Bhutan. Only Bhutan's kings and spiritual leaders are allowed to touch it.

A dragon mask worn by a monk at the coronation

Crowning glory

👑 **Big spender.** Jean Bedel Bokassa (b.1921), Emperor of the Central African Republic, spent £20 million ($31 million) on his coronation when the average wage in the country was £16.50 (about $26) a year.

A detail from Bokassa's coronation robe.

👑 **A brief rule.** The shortest ever reign was that of Crown Prince Filipe of Portugal, who was fatally wounded at the same time that his father was shot dead in Lisbon in 1908. He was technically king for about 20 minutes.

King Edward's crown

The Imperial State crown

The ring

The spurs

The sceptre

The orb

The sword

This diadem was worn by the queen before her coronation.

3. The oath – The queen swears to maintain the laws and customs of the country and to defend the Church.

4. The anointing – The queen's robes are removed. Four knights hold a canopy over her. The archbishop uses holy oil to make the sign of a cross on her body.

5. The crowning – The queen is dressed in robes and given the regalia. The archbishop places the crown on her head.

A palace is the home of the monarch and the royal family. Palaces are also used for state ceremonies, as meeting places for governments, and as holy places of religious worship. Here is a selection of some of the splendid palaces that have been built through the ages.

The hilltop palace of Masada

King Herod the Great (74-4 BC) built five great palaces. The most famous is Masada, a fortress-palace which stands on a rock 400m (1300ft) high above the Dead Sea.

A plan (above) and a side view (left) of the fortress-palace of Masada

Masada was the scene of a tragic incident in 66. A group of Jews revolted against the Romans occupying Jerusalem. Some fled to Masada and resisted attack for three years. The Romans built a huge ramp to the top of the hill and thus were able to take the fortress. The Jews inside committed suicide rather than be taken captive.

Alhambra Palace, Spain

The Alhambra Palace, built on a hill above Granada in southern Spain, was the palace of Moorish kings. The Moors were Muslim warriors who invaded Spain from North Africa in the 8th century.

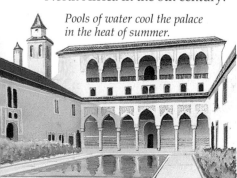

Pools of water cool the palace in the heat of summer.

The finest surviving example of Moorish architecture, the Alhambra was built in the 14th century by Yusuf I and Mohammed V. Its interiors are decorated with glazed tiles, geometric and floral patterns and scripts from the Koran.

Forbidden city

Some kings were considered too holy to be seen by ordinary people. They lived hidden behind palace walls. At different times, 24 emperors lived in the world's largest palace complex, the Forbidden City, in Beijing, China.

A Chinese illustration of part of the Forbidden City

Started in the 15th century during the reign of Emperor Yongle, the city took a million men 16 years to complete. It covers 72 hectares (177.9 acres) and has 8000 rooms, 17 palaces, halls, temples, libraries, courtyards and gardens.

The last Chinese emperor to live in the Forbidden City was Pu Yi (see page 33), who left the palace in 1924.

The city is guarded by bronze lions.

A palace for the Sun King

The splendid Palace of Versailles, built outside Paris by Louis XIV (1638-1715), became the focus of French art and culture. Its design has been copied by other monarchs.

Louis was the most powerful of all the European kings at this time.

The picture below shows the Palace of Versailles and some of its main rooms.

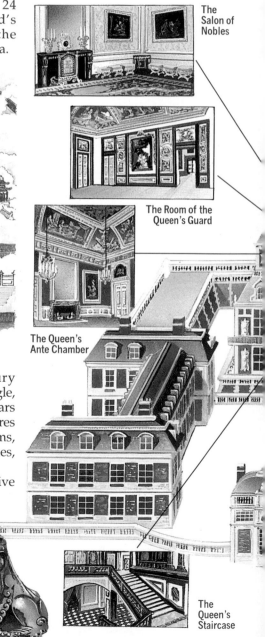

The Salon of Nobles

The Room of the Queen's Guard

The Queen's Ante Chamber

The Queen's Staircase

He reigned for 72 years, living a life of wealth and extravagance. He wanted to build a palace that reflected his glory. It took 47 years to complete Versailles, with its 1400 fountains and floors and walls of marble.

Louis XIV was known as the "Sun King"

Prinny and the Royal Pavilion

Palaces were often the product of a king's extravagant wishes. Prince George (1762-1830), who later became George IV of England, built the weird and wonderful Royal Pavilion.

Prinny, as he was known, loved Brighton, a small port on the south coast of England. He changed his villa there into a great palace called the Pavilion, which he filled with incredible furniture.

He threw extravagant parties there. At one meal, a stream with mossy banks, bridges and live goldfish, flowed down the middle of the table. When George became king in 1820, he was forced to abandon his palace and his carefree life and move back to London.

Prince George

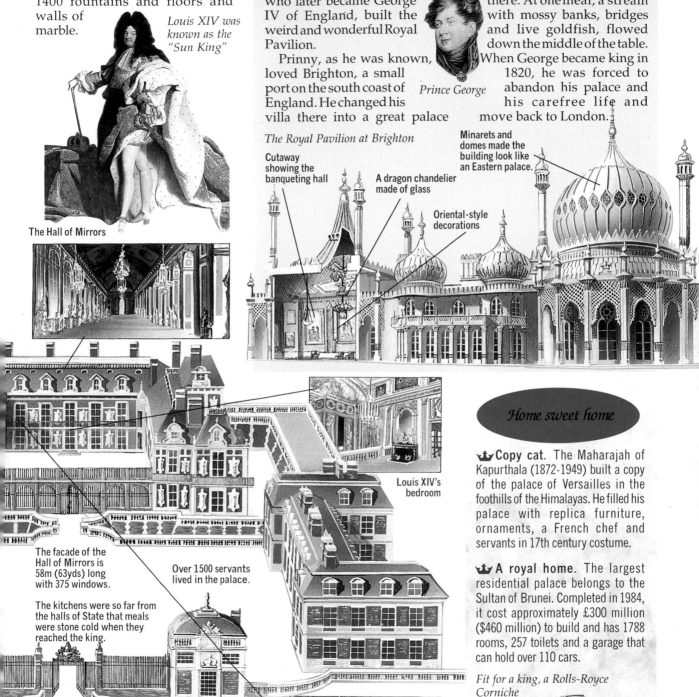

The Hall of Mirrors

The Royal Pavilion at Brighton

Cutaway showing the banqueting hall

A dragon chandelier made of glass

Minarets and domes made the building look like an Eastern palace.

Oriental-style decorations

Louis XIV's bedroom

The facade of the Hall of Mirrors is 58m (63yds) long with 375 windows.

Over 1500 servants lived in the palace.

The kitchens were so far from the halls of State that meals were stone cold when they reached the king.

There were no toilets at the palace and only a few baths. Men and women covered themselves with perfume instead of bathing.

Room of the Bull's Eye

Home sweet home

♛**Copy cat.** The Maharajah of Kapurthala (1872-1949) built a copy of the palace of Versailles in the foothills of the Himalayas. He filled his palace with replica furniture, ornaments, a French chef and servants in 17th century costume.

♛**A royal home.** The largest residential palace belongs to the Sultan of Brunei. Completed in 1984, it cost approximately £300 million ($460 million) to build and has 1788 rooms, 257 toilets and a garage that can hold over 110 cars.

Fit for a king, a Rolls-Royce Corniche

People have always gathered around monarchs, attracted by their wealth and power. The home of a ruler is called a court, and the people who live there are called courtiers. Though courtiers live lives of luxury, they depend on the generosity of a monarch for their survival.

The role of a courtier

A variety of jobs were available at a royal court. But as the number of courtiers at some palaces grew, it was increasingly difficult to find them all roles. Louis XIV of France (1638-1715) had hundreds of courtiers and gave many of them meaningless tasks to perform.

Jobs at the court of Louis XIV

Many courtiers were required to help the king dress in the morning. The sole task of one man was to hold the royal coat.

The king's elaborate wig was curled and powdered by servants, but a courtier passed it to the king when he was dressing.

Another courtier attended every meal that the king ate so that he could pass him his napkin.

Sultan Abdul Aziz of Turkey (1830-76) had more than 5000 servants at his court. The only task of one man was to cut the Sultan's fingernails when they grew too long.

Court rules

At most courts, there were strict rules outlining how courtiers should treat the royal family. At the court of the King of Siam, for instance, few people were allowed to touch the king and queen. So when a barge carrying Queen Sunanda (1860-81) overturned, the boatmen were not allowed to pull her out of the water. By the time someone of high enough rank to touch her arrived, she had drowned.

Following the fashion

Monarchs have often inspired fashions at court. Courtiers were able to flatter kings and queens by copying their appearance or style of dress.

As she grew older, Elizabeth I of England (1533-1603) wore thick white makeup on her face. Many of the women at the royal court followed her example. The white makeup contained lead, which eventually destroyed their skin.

This portrait of Elizabeth I shows many of the fashions she inspired.

Elizabeth wore thick white makeup.

The queen was famous for her red hair and high hair line.

Large ruff collars became very fashionable

During the 18th century, a hairstyle known as the "pompadour" became very fashionable at the French court. It was inspired by a style worn by Louis XV's mistress, Madame de Pompadour, that became very exaggerated.

Constructing a "pompadour" hairstyle

Pads or cages were fixed on the top of the wearer's head.

The woman's hair, or false hair, was then smoothed over the cage. Sometimes it was covered in powder.

Hairstyles were decorated with ribbons, feathers, flowers and even fruit.

In 1778, there was a sea battle in which the ship *La Belle Poule* fought the English. French women wore model boats on their hair, with cannons, sails and flags.

A hairstyle inspired by La Belle Poule

Many women did not wash their hair for months, and they often found it full of lice or even mice.

Hairstyles reached great heights.

Courtly flattery

The position of a courtier was a vulnerable one, dependent on his or her popularity with the monarch. Some people were driven to great lengths of flattery to preserve their positions. In the 17th century, the Duc d'Antin supervised the building work at Versailles, near Paris. He deliberately had some of the statues in the palace gardens placed a little askew so that he could praise Louis XIV of France when he noticed the fault.

A statue from the gardens at Versailles

Maltreating the staff

Provoking the disapproval of a monarch could have terrible consequences for some courtiers. Empress Anna of Russia (1693-1740) forced three of her courtiers to live as hens for a week. Wearing feathers, they were put in "nesting boxes" in one of the main reception halls of the palace.

Empress Anna punishes Michael Golitsin

When a prince called Michael Golitsin offended Empress Anna, she forced him to marry an ugly servant girl.

On their wedding night, the couple were locked in a palace made of ice, with guards to prevent them escaping.

Miraculously, Golitsin and his wife both survived their ordeal and she later gave birth to twin sons.

Travel within kingdoms

It was important for monarchs to tour their realms, so that they could be seen and admired by their subjects. For some rulers, travel was an opportunity to find out what was happening in their kingdoms.

In the 3rd century BC, emperors of the Mauryan empire went on journeys in golden carriages. They were accompanied by noblemen, standard bearers, musicians blowing conch shells, horses and elephants decorated with plumes and pearls.

A selection of the types of transportation some monarchs have used.

This Egyptian chair was carried on the shoulders of four servants.

A chariot used by Emperor Wu-tsung of China in the 16th century

The Royal Yacht *Britannia*, used by Queen Elizabeth II of Great Britain and Northern Ireland

An elaborately carved wooden sled, found in the grave of a Viking queen

New goblets. The court doctors of Ogadei Khan of the Mongols (a people from Central Asia) begged him to halve the number of goblets of wine he drank a day. The Khan readily agreed, but ordered his servants to bring his wine in new goblets that were twice the size of the old ones.

A funny profession. Jesters were often employed to entertain the members of a court. The last jester in England was Muckle John, who worked at the court of King Charles I (1600-49).

A tragic tale. Louis XIV's chef, Monsieur Vatel, found he was short of lobsters for a sauce. He was so terrified of offending the king that he committed suicide.

9

Gods, kings and queens

In some cultures monarchs have been closely associated with gods and goddesses. Some were thought to be deities or the children of deities, while others were thought to represent gods on earth.

Sacred kings

Many ancient societies believed that their monarchs had special powers to make crops grow and control the weather. Sometimes leaders were sacrificed to ensure the wealth and prosperity of their people. Other societies sacrificed a substitute human or animal instead of killing their leaders.

Pharaoh Ramesses II

The people of ancient Egypt held special ceremonies at which the powers of a monarch were symbolically renewed. Pharaoh Ramesses II (c.1304-1237BC) celebrated 14 of these ceremonies, which were known as the *heb sed*.

Ramesses II celebrating a heb sed

Ramesses made offerings of food, wine and flowers to all the Egyptian gods and goddesses.

The pharaoh had to perform a ceremonial run to prove he was still fit and active enough to rule his country well.

After he had completed the run, Ramesses attended a ceremony at which priests recrowned him as king.

God kings

Japanese emperors were believed to be directly descended from the sun goddess, Yamato. They held absolute political and religious power.

Emperor Hirohito (1901-89) lived as a god king until 1946, when he had to give up most of his powers and renounce his claim to divinity.

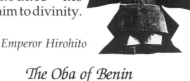

Emperor Hirohito

The Oba of Benin

Rulers of Benin (a kingdom that is now part of Nigeria) were known as Obas. All-powerful, they could command anything and expected to be obeyed immediately. They were believed to be the earthly representatives of all Benin's gods, and they were considered godlike themselves. Anyone who insulted or resisted them was executed.

An Oba of Benin and two chieftains

A ceremonial hammer

The Oba wears an oversized necklace

An ornate kilt

Decorative anklets

The rulers of Tibet

The ruler of Tibet is known as the Dalai Lama. He is both a political and religious leader. The Tibetan people follow a religion called Buddhism, and they believe that the Dalai Lama's body contains the Buddhist spirit of compassion.

Approximately 3700m (about 12,000ft) above sea level, in the Himalaya mountains, stands the palace of Potala, the traditional residence of the Dalai Lama. A popular Tibetan belief is that the palace was built by the gods in just one night. In reality, the palace that can be seen today took many years to build. Work on it began during the reign of the fifth Dalai Lama, Lobsang Gyatso (1617-82).

The palace of Potala, residence of the Dalai Lamas of Tibet

The Potala was once described as 'crowned with flames' because of its golden roofs.

The outer White Palace is so called because of its whitewashed walls.

In 1951, Tibet was occupied by the Chinese. In 1959, the 14th Dalai Lama Tenzin Gyatso (b.1935) fled to India with 80,000 followers. He continues to live in exile today.

Dalai Lama Tenzin Gyatso

Choosing a Dalai Lama

Tibetans believe that when a Dalai Lama dies, the spirit of compassion leaves his body and enters the body of a child born at exactly the same moment.

Searching for the new Dalai Lama

The dying Dalai Lama gives his monks information about where to find the baby who will be the new Dalai Lama.

The monks, who are known as "lamas", travel throughout the mountains of Tibet looking for the special child.

There are tests which help the monks in their search. For example, the baby will recognize the belongings of the previous Dalai Lama.

The inner Red Palace contains a monastery, chapels, shrines, libraries, and golden pagodas containing the embalmed bodies of previous Dalai Lamas.

Ruling with divine approval

Emperors of China during the Sang Dynasty (17-11th century BC) claimed to be descended from Shang Di, the high god of Heaven. They used the title "Son of Heaven", and were considered responsible for bringing order and harmony to Earth.

The emperors were said to rule with the "Mandate of Heaven". This meant that the gods approved of the emperors and their actions.

A Chinese emperor in traditional robes

Divine right

In the 17th century, many European kings and queens believed they had been specially chosen by God. They claimed it was their "divine right" to rule, and that they were responsible to God alone for their actions. James I of England (1566-1625) and his son Charles I both firmly believed in the "Divine Right of Kings". They argued that nobody had the right to question their decisions or actions. This view was challenged by some of their subjects and finally provoked a civil war. This led to the execution of Charles I in 1649.

James I

Divine deeds

♛ **Death wish.** In the 17th century, a sailor ran the King of Siam's barge onto a sand bank. The sailor was so horrified at having endangered his divine leader, that he insisted on being executed.

♛ **Healing hands.** The French and English believed that victims of a skin disease called scrofula (known as the "King's Evil") could be cured by the touch of a monarch's hand. The last British monarch asked to perform this treatment was Queen Anne (1665-1714).

Queen Anne

In the past, kings were expected to lead their armies into battle themselves. Many were barely competent military leaders, but some were inspired warriors who protected their realms from invasion and extended their frontiers to create vast empires.

A warrior pharaoh

The Egyptian pharaoh Tuthmosis III (15th century BC) was trained to be a soldier from a young age. He was an imaginative and resourceful leader, who led 17 military campaigns in the Middle East and Nubia. His success in battle helped create the greatest empire of the day.

A contemporary picture of Tuthmosis III in his chariot

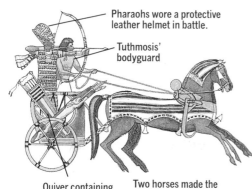

Pharaohs wore a protective leather helmet in battle.

Tuthmosis' bodyguard

Quiver containing extra arrows

Two horses made the chariot move quickly.

The mighty Khan

Temuchin (c.1162-1227) was the son of a minor chief of the Mongols, a people from Central Asia. As a young man he led a small group of followers on military raids. Success earned him the title Genghis Khan, meaning "Universal Leader". He made the Mongols a formidable fighting force, conquering an empire that spread from northern China to the Black Sea and took two years to ride across.

A persian miniature showing Genghis Khan on horseback

Alexander the Great

Alexander (356-323BC), King of Macedonia (now Greece), proved his ability on military expeditions while a teenager. He was a tactical genius, outclassing his enemies in battles, sieges and surprise attacks.

A mosaic depicting Alexander in battle

A map showing Alexander's empire

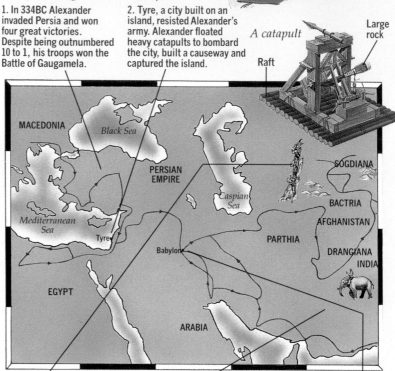

1. In 334BC Alexander invaded Persia and won four great victories. Despite being outnumbered 10 to 1, his troops won the Battle of Gaugamela.

2. Tyre, a city built on an island, resisted Alexander's army. Alexander floated heavy catapults to bombard the city, built a causeway and captured the island.

A catapult — Large rock — Raft

3. In 328BC Alexander came to the rock on which King Oxyartes had a fortress. Alexander's men drove iron pegs into the rock face. They attached rope ladders, climbed up and conquered the city.

4. When they reached India in 326BC, Alexander's men won a fierce battle against Rajah Porus. Porus gave him hundreds of elephants.

5. Exhausted, Alexander's troops refused to go on. Alexander was forced to march for home. Taken ill at a banquet in Babylon, he died in 323BC.

Akbar the Great

Akbar (1542-1605) was the greatest of a series of Indian emperors known as the Moguls. In the early years of his reign he crushed rebels within his own empire. Turning to foreign campaigns, he gradually conquered an empire covering most of northern India. The firmness and wisdom with which he governed his empire earned him the title "Guardian of Mankind."

Akbar (on the second elephant) pursuing his enemies

Frederick the Great

Frederick II of Prussia (1712-86) devoted himself to a military career. Victories against the French and the Austrians enabled him to double the size of his kingdom. His brilliant strategies and great courage earned him a reputation as a formidable military leader.

A Prussian infantryman

One of his great victories was at the Battle of Rossbach on November 5, 1757. In less than an hour 22,000 Prussians overcame 50,000 French and German troops. The Prussians took 6000 prisoners and 72 guns, losing only 300 men in the process. The picture below shows both armies engaged in battle.

A contemporary picture of Frederick's victory at the Battle of Rossbach

Zulu warrior

Shaka (c.1787-1828) was leader of the Zulu kingdom. He organized the army of 40,000 men into uniformed regiments called *impi*, and trained them rigorously. He managed to extend his kingdom over much of southern Africa.

Shaka introduced the stabbing spear

Shaka taught his men to use their shields and stabbing spears in a one-to-one attack.

A warrior hooked his shield around his opponent's, and pulled it out of the way.

This enabled him to use the stabbing spear to wound the unprotected man.

Fighting men

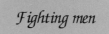

♛ **Attila the Hun**. Attila (c.406-453) was the king of an Asian tribe called the Huns. Known as the "Scourge of God", he mercilessly conquered many countries in Eastern Europe.

Attila the Hun

♛ **God's warrior**. Charlemagne, King of the Franks (747-814), led military campaigns to unite Western Europe under his control and spread Christianity.

Charlemagne

♛ **A great victory**. In 1415 Henry V of England (1387-1422) invaded France. Though outnumbered, his lightly armed archers managed to shoot the heavily armed French knights with ease, and so secure victory at the Battle of Agincourt.

A portrait of Henry V

The Prussian cavalry repeatedly charged the enemy until they broke and ran.

The Prussian infantry

The combined forces of the French and German army numbered 50,000 men (shown in red).

The 22,000 Prussians were outnumbered 2 to 1 by the French and German soldiers.

The town of Rossbach

The French and German cavalry retreated in disorder.

The Prussian artillery supported the cavalry.

Warrior queens

Traditionally, fighting was not considered a woman's role, and queens were only expected to make speeches to rally troops. Some female monarchs, however, led brave and ruthless military campaigns.

Vengeance for Queen Boudicca

Few military leaders have been able to challenge successfully the might of the Roman army, but Queen Boudicca inflicted major defeats on their ranks.

In 60, the Romans occupied much of Britain. They seized the land of King Prasutagus of the Iceni tribe. His queen, Boudicca (1st century), was captured and beaten in public and his daughters were humiliated.

The type of chariot used by Boudicca and the Iceni tribe

Many people wrongly believe that the wheels of Boudicca's chariot had blades attached to them.

Seeking her revenge, Boudicca launched a ferocious attack on Roman settlements at Colchester, St. Albans and London. Her army burned the towns to the ground, killing up to 70,000 Romans.

Eventually, the Romans rallied their forces and defeated Boudicca and her army, killing 80,000 Iceni warriors. Boudicca (and probably her daughters too) took poison rather than be captured.

Zenobia, queen of the East

Zenobia (3rd century), was a noble Arab lady. She was married to the king of the city of Palmyra, Syria (part of the Roman empire). She often joined her husband on military expeditions, riding or walking with his troops.

When Zenobia's husband was murdered in 267, she ruled until her son was old enough to inherit the throne himself. Zenobia infuriated the Romans, conquering their territory in Egypt, Syria and Asia Minor (now part of Turkey).

A fashionable costume at Zenobia's court

The Romans had taken control of Palmyra, but Zenobia announced that the city was independent of Rome. In retaliation, a Roman army, led by Emperor Aurelian, attacked the city. Zenobia and her bodyguards escaped on camels, but were arrested attempting to cross the River Euphrates to safety.

In Rome, Zenobia was paraded in Aurelian's victory celebration. Despite this humiliation, she survived. She married a Roman Senator and lived in luxury.

Aurelian's victory celebration in Rome

Elephants

Giraffes

Tigers

Elks

Gladiators

Zenobia weighed down by chains made of solid gold.

Ambassadors

Queen of the waves

In the 5th century BC, Queen Artemisia of Halicarnassus (now in Turkey) took five warships to join King Xerxes of Persia when he invaded Greece. During a naval battle off the coast of the island of Salamis, Artemisia was being pursued by her Greek enemies. She found her escape route blocked by the ship of one of her allies, so she decided to ram the ship to ensure her own escape.

Artemisia's ship ramming another Persian ship

A bronze ram sinks the ship.

People believed that these eyes scared enemies and helped the ship find its way.

The stern of the ship was decorated with a carved dragon's head.

Artemisia giving orders to her crew.

The ships shown in this picture are called triremes.

Two steering oars were used to control the ship's direction.

The oars were over 4m (14ft) long.

Platform for archers and spearmen

Spearman

Protected by a row of shields, a spearman fired at the enemy and tried to board their ship.

Experts think that the oarsmen sat three deep, but we do not know exactly how these ships were rowed.

Matilda, the queen who was never crowned

In 1120, the only son of King Henry I of England (1068-1135) drowned in a shipwreck. This left Henry's daughter Matilda (1102-67) as the only heir to the throne. The king made his nobles swear to support and follow Matilda when she was queen. But only three weeks after Henry died, his nephew Stephen seized the throne of England.

Matilda waged war on Stephen to win back the crown. She quickly proved to be a more able and ruthless leader than her opponent. For example, when Stephen's forces captured Matilda, the chivalrous king agreed to release her. But when she captured Stephen in a later battle, Matilda had him put in chains and humiliated. She declared herself "Lady of the English".

A contemporary picture of Matilda

Matilda went to London to be crowned, but she was very unpopular with many people. Her determination and courage were considered unnatural in a woman. On the eve of her coronation, the people of London rose up against her, and she was forced to flee to Normandy, France.

Stephen gradually regained power in England and so, despite her efforts, Matilda was never crowned Queen of England.

There are many stories of how Matilda avoided capture by Stephen's troops.

Once Matilda pretended to be dead and managed to get away from her enemies on a cart which carried coffins.

On another occasion she escaped a besieged castle during a blizzard by dressing in white and slipping past enemy soldiers.

During the blizzard Matilda was able to escape her pursuers by walking across the River Thames, which was frozen at the time.

👑 **Rest in peace.** One legend claims that Queen Boudicca is buried under platform eight of Kings Cross, a railway station in London.

👑 **Three golden flies.** While acting as regent for her son, Queen Ahhotep (16th century BC) led an army against rebels. She was later presented with three golden flies, Egypt's highest award for bravery.

Ahhotep's golden flies

👑 **Jinga the queen.** Some say Jinga Mbandi (c.1580-1663) killed her brother to become Queen of Matamba, West Africa. She negotiated independence for her kingdom with the Portuguese governor. When Portuguese troops drove her out, she trained soldiers herself and fought back repeatedly.

The Portuguese governor did not offer a chair, so Jinga sat on a servant.

👑 **Historical confusion.** Amanirenas, queen mother of the Kingdom of Meroë in Africa, led a successful attack on Roman garrisons in southern Egypt in 7BC. Roman historians called her Candace, which was not her name but her title.

👑 **The Rebel Rani.** In 1857 Lakshimbai, the Rani of the kingdom of Jhansi, joined rebel leaders in a revolt against the British who occupied India. She died fighting, but a British general admitted that she was a very brave and dangerous opponent.

The Rebel Rani wore jodhpurs and jewels in battle.

Royal builders

Many kings and queens commissioned buildings during their reigns. But some royal builders overshadowed the rest, erecting castles, great temples, vast fortifications and even entire cities.

The great pyramids

Several Egyptian pharaohs erected massive monuments called pyramids, to mark their future burial places. The largest is that of King Khufu who ruled in the 25th century BC.

Constructing Khufu's pyramid

2.3 million blocks were cut from quarries. Each weighed about 23,000kg (50,000lbs). They were floated across the River Nile.

Ramps made of rubble were used to raise the blocks above ground level. Wooden poles were used to lever them into position.

As the pyramid grew higher, the ramps were made longer. The pyramid was finally covered in white limestone to make it shiny.

Inside the pyramid

Air shaft

Burial chamber

Workmen's passages

Ramesses' temple

Pharaoh Ramesses II (c.1304-1237BC) undertook many massive building projects during his reign. Egyptian poets praised the beauty of Per-Ramesses, the new city he built. He constructed a chain of fortresses to protect Egypt from the people of Libya, and built spectacular tombs and temples. His most famous building is the great temple at Abu Simbel.

Vast statues of Ramesses II sit outside the temple of Abu Simbel.

Building the city of Babylon

Babylon, the capital city of Babylonia (now part of modern Iraq), was built by Nebuchadnezzar II in the 6th century BC.

A reconstruction of the city of Babylon

This temple platform, called a ziggurat, was built by Nebuchadnezzar for a god named Marduk.

It was the richest and most magnificent city of its time. Two massive walls 18m (60ft) high, stretching for 13km (8 miles), enclosed the temples and palaces of the inner city. When the site was excavated in the 19th century, the only part of the city still standing was a gateway. This is known as the Ishtar Gate, after the goddess Ishtar to whom it is dedicated.

Nebuchadnezzar married a princess named Amytis. When she became homesick for the hills of her homeland, he built gardens to remind her of them. Now known as the "Hanging Gardens of Babylon", they were built on steep terraces to imitate hillsides. Machinery raised water to the gardens from a nearby river.

A statue of the goddess Ishtar

The walls of Nebuchadnezzar's throne room were 3m (10ft) thick to combat temperatures that reached 55°C (131°F).

The gardens were said to be one of the Seven Wonders of the Ancient World.

The Ishtar Gate, decorated with glazed blue tiles depicting bulls and dragons

The Great Wall of China

When Zheng (259-210BC) became king of the province of Qin he united China under his rule. He took the name Shih Huang Ti, which means "First Emperor of China".

He wanted to construct a wall to protect China from its enemies. Slaves, prisoners and peasants were forced to work in harsh conditions to build the wall. Many thousands of them died.

Shih Huang Ti

The Great Wall is the largest man-made structure in the world, and can be seen by astronauts orbiting the Earth. But it did not serve its purpose and was penetrated by many different invaders. The Mongol leader Genghis Khan is believed to have bribed guards on the wall to allow his army into China.

This picture shows the Great Wall in the last stages of its construction.

The wall varies from 4.5-12m (15-39ft) thick and is up to 9.8m (32ft) high.

Towers were built at regular intervals. They housed 4-5 soldiers.

Existing earth walls were joined together, and strengthened with stones.

A map showing the extent of the Great Wall

MONGOLIA

TIBET

Great Wall

CHINA

INDIA

There are 6320km (4000 miles) of wall.

If workers died, their bodies were built into the wall.

Peter the Great

Tsar Peter the Great of Russia (1672-1725) wanted to build a new city, St. Petersburg, at the mouth of the River Neva. He wanted to make it as great as any city in Europe, so he visited Germany, England and Holland, and took architects, crafts-men and artists back to Russia.

As the site was wet and marshy, building the city was difficult. Timbers had to be driven into marshland, forests were cleared and hills flattened.

Peter the Great

👑 **Modern method.** An estimated 4000 workers spent 40 years building the pyramid of King Khufu. In 1974, experts calculated that, with modern equipment, it would take 405 workmen only six years.

These hieroglyphs mean "Khufu"

👑 **Big thinker.** Sultan Moulay Ismail of Morocco (1672-1727) built a royal city with walls 40km (25 miles) long, 50 palaces, and a stable which could accommodate 12,000 horses.

👑 **A city in the clouds.** The city at Machu Picchu, probably built by Emperor Pachacuti of Peru (1438-71), stands an incredible 600m (2000ft) up on a peak in the Andes.

Machu Picchu

An obsessive builder

Ludwig II of Bavaria (1845-86) had a passion for building. During his reign, he spent vast sums from the treasury constructing two castles and three palaces, at a time when Bavaria was in financial difficulty. By 1886, Ludwig's obsession had brought his country massive debts.

Neuschwanstein castle was built by Christian Jank, a theatrical designer.

The castle was built on the top of a mountain.

Most of the castle was made of white limestone.

Red sandstone gatehouse

Monarchs have often surrounded themselves with very gifted people. While some rulers were talented in their own right, others became famous as patrons (people who finance and support craftsmen, artists, scholars and explorers).

Henry the Navigator

Prince Henry of Portugal (1394-1460) devoted his life to discovery. As Governor of the Algarve, in Portugal, he built a shipyard and a school to train navigators and pilots. He recruited many mariners, astronomers and geographers, and inspired his courtiers to lead expeditions to explore the west coast of Africa. Henry sent out 14 expeditions, but each one turned back before rounding Cape Bojador. The sailors believed that beyond this point lay the "Green Sea of Darkness", where the sun burned people's skins black, the sea boiled and there were whirlpools and thick green fogs where monsters lurked. It was not until 1434 that courtier Gil Eannes sailed beyond the Cape and survived to tell the tale.

Henry the Navigator

A Portuguese ship, and a map of Eannes' route round the west coast of Africa

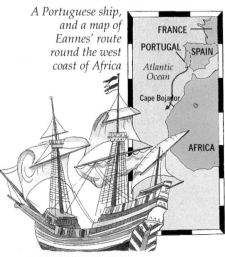

FRANCE
PORTUGAL SPAIN
Atlantic Ocean
Cape Bojador
AFRICA

Culture at court

Elizabeth I of England (1533-1603) spoke five languages, and had a passion for riding, music, dancing and poetry. When a diplomat from Scotland boasted to Elizabeth that Mary, Queen of Scots, was an accomplished musician, Elizabeth went to the virginal (a keyboard instrument) to prove that she too could play brilliantly.

Queen Elizabeth playing the lute

Elizabeth's court attracted many talented authors and artists. William Shakespeare (1564-1616) wrote his play *Twelfth Night* to be performed for the queen in 1599.

Shakespeare's plays were performed at The Globe

Portrait of a king

In 1632, Charles I of England (1600-49) invited the Flemish painter Anthony Van Dyck (1599-1641) to court. Van Dyck's portraits so impressed the king that he gave the artist a knighthood and a pension to encourage him to stay in England. The artist's style had a great influence on portrait painting in England for two centuries.

A portrait of Charles I by Van Dyck

The building had no roof. If it rained, plays were called off.

Galleries above the stage were used for balcony scenes.

The walls have been cutaway to show wealthy guests and musicians sitting in wooden galleries.

It cost only a penny to stand in front of the stage and watch.

Pompadour porcelain

Madame de Pompadour (1721-64), mistress of Louis XV of France, passionately supported the arts. She encouraged writers, and persuaded Louis to patronize the finest artists, craftsmen and architects of his day.

The Sèvres porcelain factory owes its survival to La Pompadour. She asked the king to invest in the factory, and promote its products by making them fashionable at the Royal court.

Sèvres porcelain

Ludwig II and Wagner

The German composer Richard Wagner (1813-83) was in serious financial trouble when he was summoned to the court of King Ludwig II of Bavaria (1845-86). The king loved Wagner's music and promised to pay him a vast salary.

Wagner was quick to take advantage of the king's generosity. Once, when police arrived at Wagner's apartment to seize his possessions as security for his debts, Wagner sent a friend to the king's treasury and was able to pay the debt with 2400 florins.

The Swan King from a Wagner opera

Bavarian ministers hated Wagner, accusing him of meddling in politics. The final insult came when Wagner attacked the government in an article. Ludwig was forced to banish him from Bavaria.

Richard Wagner

Fabergé eggs

The customers of the craftsman Carl Fabergé (1846-1920) included many European monarchs and aristocrats. His greatest customer was Tsar Nicholas II of Russia.

In 1884, Fabergé was asked to make an Easter egg for the tsar's wife. Over the following years a total of 56 decorated eggs were delivered to the palace at Easter.

A selection of eggs made by Carl Fabergé

This egg is decorated with jewels. The picture of the tsar's children fits inside.

(left) This egg is a clock with a vase of lilies. The numbers on the clock are studded with diamonds and a golden arrow shows the time.

(below) These lilies of the valley are made from pearls and rose-diamonds, with gold and emerald leaves.

(below) This egg is decorated with imperial eagles and diamonds. A working model of the tsar's coronation coach fits inside.

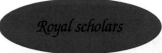

👑 **A soldier's thoughts.** Emperor Marcus Aurelius (121-80) of Rome was constantly fighting to protect the frontiers of the Roman Empire, but he found time to study literature, philosophy and law. "Meditations", a record of his innermost thoughts, is still studied today.

A coin showing Marcus Aurelius

👑 **A royal composer.** Henry VIII of England (1491-1547) was an accomplished musician. He played the organ, virginal and the harp. Some people think he may have written the famous tune "Greensleeves".

A miniature showing Henry playing the harp.

👑 **Pen name for a queen.** Queen Elizabeth of Rumania (1843-1916) published her poems and fairy stories using the pen name Carmen Sylva.

👑 **A late starter.** Charlemagne (747-814), King of the Franks, did not learn to write until he was an adult. However, he founded schools and gathered some of Europe's greatest scholars at his court.

Charlemagne encouraged very high standards in art, architecture and craftsmanship.

A bust of Emperor Charlemagne. His name means "Charles the Great".

Tragic monarchs

Assassination by enemies has always been one of the greatest hazards of leadership. Some monarchs were executed by rivals, while others perished at the hands of their own subjects.

The last Aztec emperor

The Aztecs were a race of people who inhabited Mexico from about 1325. In 1519, a group of Spanish adventurers, who are known as the *Conquistadors*, landed on the coast of Mexico. They reached a city called Tenochtitlán, the capital of the Aztec empire. They were led there by a native woman known as Malinche, who had fallen in love with Hernando Cortés, the leader of the Spanish troops.

When the Spanish arrived, the Aztecs thought that they were gods and worshipped them. But Cortés ruthlessly imprisoned the Aztec king, Montezuma (1466-1519).

When a rebellion broke out among the Aztecs, Montezuma was brought out to calm his people. But he had never been a popular leader, and the crowd showered him with stones and arrows. He died from his injuries soon after.

Queen for 1000 days

Henry VIII of England (see page 24) desperately wanted a son to inherit his throne. When his second wife Anne Boleyn (c.1504-36) had a baby girl, he began to tire of her.

Anne was overjoyed when she became pregnant again. But she miscarried the baby, a boy, when shocked by stories suggesting the king had had a serious accident.

Henry believed that Anne had failed him, and put her on trial. Despite her innocence, she was found guilty of adultery and beheaded. Only 11 days later, Henry married Jane Seymour.

Anne Boleyn

A hired assassin

Philip II of Spain controlled the Netherlands. A devout Catholic, he persecuted Dutch Protestants until they revolted. They were led by William, Prince of Orange (1533-84). Philip offered a reward to anyone willing to murder the prince.

Prince William of Orange

Balthassar Gérards, a cabinet-maker's apprentice, boasted that he would kill William. In disguise, he went to the prince, who gave him a job. Gérards then bought a pair of pistols and killed William as he was about to dine. Gérards was executed, but Philip paid the reward to his family.

The Spaniards attack Tenochtitlán

The Aztecs had never seen horses or cannons and were terrified.

Temple of the Feathered Serpent, one of the Aztec gods

Temple of the Rain God

Temple of the War God, the chief Aztec god

An Aztec warrior

Leopardskin tunic

Wooden spear

Shield covered in feathers

Metal breast plate over chain mail tunic

Battle axe

A Spanish Conquistador

This portrait of King Montezuma is by an Aztec artist. The royal standard of feathers from the Quetzalcoatl bird is strapped to the king's back.

Tried and executed

Charles I (1600-49) is the only English king to have been executed. During his reign, a war broke out between king and Parliament. Parliament wanted more say in matters of religion, finance and foreign policy, but Charles considered it his right to decide upon these matters.

In 1649 the king was captured, tried for treason and sentenced to death. The day of his execution was a cold one, so Charles wore two shirts. He did not want onlookers to think he was shivering with fear when he walked out to face the executioner's axe.

A contemporary picture showing the execution of Charles I of England

The queen of luxury

Marie Antoinette (1755-93) was the wife of Louis XVI of France (1754-93). She was notorious for her frivolity and extravagance. Living in luxury at the Palace of Versailles, she gave no thought to the suffering of the poor. Because of this, she became a focus for the French people's hatred of the monarchy.

When revolution broke out, Marie Antoinette and Louis tried to flee France, but they were intercepted, brought back to Paris and imprisoned. Louis was tried and executed in 1793 and Marie Antoinette followed him to the guillotine nine months later.

A sketch of Marie Antoinette on her way to the guillotine

How the guillotine was used

During the French Revolution, any man or woman suspected of being unpatriotic was sent to the guillotine. The prisoner was brought to the platform.

The prisoner was forced to lie on a wooden bench. The blade of the guillotine was raised, using a rope. When the rope was pulled, the blade fell, cutting the head off.

The head was caught in a basket. Sometimes it was lifted up to show the crowd.

The guillotine

The heavy blade fell quickly when the rope was pulled.

A rope was used to raise and lower the blade.

The prisoner's head was secured between these two pieces of wood.

Executing the Romanovs

Tsar Nicholas Romanov II of Russia (1868-1918) and his family lived in wealth and luxury until the Russian Revolution broke out in 1917 and he was forced to abdicate.

The Romanovs were imprisoned at a town called Yekaterinburg. On July 16, 1918, the tsar's supporters were nearing the town. The revolutionaries could not risk the tsar being rescued. In the middle of the night, the family were taken to a cellar and executed by a firing squad. Their bodies were taken away and disposed of.

Bones belonging to the tsar, his empress and three of their five children were found in 1991.

A photograph of the Romanov family

Tragic but true

♛ **A dish of mushrooms.** To ensure her son became the next emperor of Rome, Agrippina poisoned her husband, Emperor Claudius (10BC-54), with a dish of mushrooms. She also had his eldest son, Britannicus, murdered.

A bust of Claudius

♛ **A king's ransom.** The largest ransom ever was paid to Spanish adventurers by the Inca people of Peru in 1533. They filled a room with gold (the equivalent of $170 million) in return for the life of their leader Atahualpa. But the Spaniards still strangled Atahualpa.

King Atahualpa

Pious monarchs

F ew kings and queens have resisted the luxuries that a life of great wealth and power can offer. But some rulers managed to live according to strict religious principles, piously devoting themselves to their chosen faiths.

Akhenaten

As a young man, Amenhotep IV (14th century BC) began to worship Aten, the sun god. When he became a pharaoh, he changed his name to Akhenaten, which means "living spirit of Aten".

Akhenaten banned the worship of all other gods and goddesses and built a city, called Akhetaten, as a tribute to Aten.

The king's subjects missed the old deities and soon went back to worshipping them when the king died. Later, they called him the "criminal of Akhetaten".

A statue of Akhenaten

From slaughter to prayer

Asoka, king of the Mauryan empire in India, led his army to war in 273BC. Hundreds of thousands of men were slaughtered. The sight of the dead and dying appalled Asoka so much that he became a Buddhist. Buddhism is a religion which teaches its followers the importance of destroying greed, hatred and delusion.

Buddhism became the official religion throughout Asoka's empire. He sent out missionaries to spread its teachings. In Sri Lanka, they managed to convert the king and court.

One of many columns erected by King Asoka

Julian, the pious pagan

When the Roman emperor Constantine the Great died in 337, his three sons inherited the throne. All the male members of his family considered a threat to the throne were murdered. Constantine's nephew Julian (c.331-363) was spared because he was only a child. But he lost his father, brother, uncle and cousins. The tragedy turned Julian against Christianity, the faith in which he had been raised.

When he became emperor in 361, Julian devoted himself to the Roman gods and goddesses and rebuilt their temples.

Christianity was restored after Julian died and he became known as Julian the "Apostate" (someone who abandons one religion for another).

Emperor Julian dressed as a god

A selection of the Roman gods and goddesses that Julian worshipped

Jupiter, king of the gods
Juno, goddess of women
Vesta, goddess of the home
Neptune, god of the sea
Dis, god of the underworld
Ceres, goddess of agriculture
Vulcan, god of craftsmen

Mars, god of war
Diana, goddess of hunting
Apollo, god of the sun
Minerva, goddess of wisdom
Mercury, Jupiter's messenger
Bacchus, god of wine
Venus, goddess of love

Saint Olaf

Viking warrior Olaf Haraldsson (c.995-1030) began sailing the Baltic Sea at the age of 12. He led many raids in Europe, and even pulled down London Bridge with grappling irons in 1010.

Olaf returned home to Norway, and was converted to Christianity. When he became king, he forced his subjects to become Christians, often offering death as their only alternative. Olaf was killed in battle, but people claimed to see miracles at his grave. Later he became Norway's first saint.

A manuscript illumination showing Olaf being killed at the Battle of Stiklestad.

Vladimir the saint

Ruler Vladimir (c.956-1015) killed one of his brothers in the struggle to become ruler of the kingdom of Kiev (now part of Russia). Once in power, he kept 800 concubines in his palace, and even encouraged human sacrifices.

A very shrewd politician, Vladimir won rich trading contacts with the city of Byzantium (now Istanbul) by becoming a Christian. He forced his subjects to undergo mass baptisms and built churches throughout Russia. Despite his often violent actions, Vladimir was later made a saint for converting so many people to Christianity.

Vladimir the saint

Priests were sent from Byzantium to baptize Vladimir's subjects.

Saint Clotilda

Clotilda was the niece of the King of Burgundy. In 493 she married Clovis, King of the Franks. Clotilda became famous for her great piety and her good works.

It is said that Clovis decided to become a Christian during a battle. While fighting, he began thinking of his wife and won a victory. Clotilda was later made a saint.

Statues of Clotilda and Clovis from the church of Notre Dame de Corbeil, France

Saint Louis, the crusader

Louis IX of France (1215-70) was a strong king and a deeply religious man. During an illness he vowed to join one of the Crusades, a series of military expeditions by European Christians to regain the Holy Land (Palestine) from the Turks.

Louis led the sixth Crusade (1248-54), but he was soon taken prisoner and was held until a large ransom was paid. In 1270 he set off again, but died of plague at Tunis in North Africa. He was declared a saint in 1297.

Louis IX of France

The side of this Crusade galleon has been cut away to show the stables inside

Holier-than-thou

Saint Margaret. A young Anglo-Saxon princess named Margaret wanted to be a nun, but the Scottish king Malcolm III insisted that she marry him instead. Margaret encouraged her husband to build monasteries and to make changes in the Scottish Church. She was made a saint in 1251.

The Confessor. Edward, King of England (c.1003-66) was such a devoted Christian that he gained the name "the Confessor". He built Westminster Abbey, where he was buried in 1066.

Edward shown in the tapestry called the Bayeux Tapestry

A lookout stood in this crow's-nest.

The Crusaders' flag was decorated with a cross.

The main sails are folded away.

Cabin for the king

The horses were led up a ramp.

Stables

Crusaders waiting to board the vessel.

23

Since the earliest times, people at royal courts have plotted and schemed to achieve their political aims. Indeed, in his book *The Prince*, a 16th-century Italian statesman called Machiavelli advised rulers to be prepared to commit evil acts to secure power.

A harem conspiracy

Some societies have allowed kings to have many wives. This often led to intrigues, conspiracies and murders as wives competed with each other for supremacy.

At the court of Ramesses III (1198-1167BC) one of his wives, Tiy, began plotting to ensure her son inherited the throne. 29 courtiers and several army officers helped her.

The conspiracy against Ramesses III

The court conspirators made several attacks on the pharaoh. They attempted to hijack his royal barge.

They used witchcraft to try to harm Ramesses III. Finally they openly attacked him, but were captured by the royal guard.

The conspirators were put on trial. Some were flogged or had their noses cut off, others were executed. Tiy and her son were allowed to commit suicide.

Herod, a family man

When the Romans gave the throne of Judea (now in Israel) to Herod the Great (74-4BC), it was unpopular with the Judeans. Herod often feared that people with a better claim to the throne would plot against him. In 29BC he married a Jewish princess called Mariamne. But he had her brother drowned and her grandfather strangled, believing that they wanted to seize his throne. When Mariamne showed anger at his deeds, Herod falsely charged her with adultery and she was executed.

Fiendish Fredegond

In the 6th century, King Chilperic of Neustria (which is now part of France) fell in love with a servant girl named Fredegond. She is believed to have strangled Chilperic's first wife so that she could marry the king herself.

King Chilperic of Neustria

When Fredegond had a son, she murdered Chilperic's other children in order to ensure that her son would inherit the crown.

The king refused to believe Fredegond was guilty, but in 584 he himself was killed, probably on the queen's orders. Fredegond ruled successfully on her son's behalf until her death in 597.

Vlad the Impaler

Vlad was a 15th century prince of Wallachia (in modern Romania). He became infamous for impaling enemy soldiers and many of his own citizens on sharpened sticks. As a result he became known as "Vlad the Impaler", and was feared and hated. During a war against Turkey, Vlad's men turned against him and killed him. The legend of Dracula the vampire is based on Vlad, whose father was named Vlad Drakul.

A modern image of Dracula

Henry VIII and his six wives

The lengths to which Henry VIII of England (1491-1547) went to get a male heir amazed Europe. In 1509, he married Catherine of Aragon. When all her sons died in infancy, Henry wanted his marriage declared invalid. The Pope refused, so Henry cut ties between England and the Catholic Church.

Catherine of Aragon

He then married Anne Boleyn, with whom he was already in love. But when she could not provide a son he had her executed for alleged infidelity.

Anne Boleyn

The king seemed to be genuinely fond of his third wife, Jane Seymour. But she died giving birth to a baby boy. The child was Henry's first male heir to survive infancy. His name was Edward and he was a weak, sickly child. He died at the age of 16 after he had reigned for only six years.

Jane Seymour

Henry VIII, as painted by Hans Holbein

The portrait was painted in 1537 when Henry was 28 years old and at the height of his power.

Henry is shown with extremely wide shoulders and his feet placed apart to emphasize his power and importance.

Henry's cloak is decorated with fur and gold thread.

The wealth of Henry's clothes and jewels were intended to reflect his success.

At the beginning of his reign Henry was tall and handsome, but he became grossly overweight and suffered with terrible ulcers on his bloated legs.

Henry divorced wife number four, Anne of Cleves, after only six months. At the age of 55 he fell in love with Catherine Howard, a teenager. But she was unfaithful to him and he had her executed.

Anne of Cleves (left)

Catherine Howard (right)

Henry's sixth wife, Catherine Parr, just managed to escape the executioner's blade. Henry died before he could sentence her to death.

Catherine Parr

Brotherly love

When the Sultan of the Ottoman Empire died, his son Mahomet III (1566-1603) was determined to get rid of rival claimants to his throne.

How Mahomet safeguarded his throne

Within hours of his father dying, Mahomet summoned his younger brothers. Led by the eldest who was eleven, the boys kissed Mahomet's hand.

Mahomet ordered guards to take the boys away into a room behind the throne room, where they were all strangled.

Mahomet also drowned seven ladies from his father's harem because they were pregnant and their children would have been potential rivals.

The diamond necklace affair

Jeanne de Motte was an ambitious countess who lived at the French royal court in the 18th century. She devised a plan to make her fortune. She knew that a man named Cardinal de Rohan desperately wanted to win the approval of the queen, Marie Antoinette. She pretended to Rohan that the queen had requested his help to buy a diamond necklace. But once Rohan had acquired the necklace, Jeanne stole it and gave it to her husband to sell.

When the craftsman who had made the necklace received no payment, he went to the queen. The queen refused to pay for something she had never even ordered.

Eventually the plot was revealed and Jeanne was imprisoned.

The necklace which caused a scandal

It contained 540 perfect diamonds.

It's scandalous!

A blind rage. An 18th century Shah of Persia had 20,000 people from the city of Kerman blinded when they refused to bow down to him. The Shah was assassinated in 1797.

No entry. The future George IV of England and his wife Caroline of Brunswick had a very unhappy marriage. Their relationship became so strained that when George was crowned, Caroline was actually turned away from the coronation ceremony.

Caroline of Brunswick

Royal marriages were usually arranged for political reasons rather than for love. Some monarchs struggled to be allowed to marry partners of their choice. Others made disastrous marriages and were forced to look for love elsewhere.

Antony and Cleopatra

Queen Cleopatra of Egypt (69-30BC) was said to be so beautiful that she brought chaos to the Roman Empire. She set out to win the love of a Roman general named Mark Antony. She sailed to meet him on a magnificent barge and entertained him with banquets and great luxury. Antony soon divorced his first wife and married Cleopatra.

Cleopatra (above) and Antony

Octavian, the brother of Mark Antony's first wife, declared war on Antony and Cleopatra. In 31BC the Egyptian fleet was defeated at Actium, off the coast of Africa. Antony committed suicide, by falling on his sword. Cleopatra is said to have held a snake to her breast and died from its venom.

This reconstruction shows Cleopatra arriving in a royal barge to meet Mark Antony.

The royal barge could travel under sail or powered by the oarsmen.

The barge docked on the banks of the River Nile.

The queen's royal cabin

Queen Cleopatra

Mark Antony

Crowning the dead

In 1359, Dom Pedro (1334-69), son of Alfonso XI of Portugal, married Inez de Castro. The couple kept their marriage a secret because Alfonso disapproved of Inez. When he discovered the truth, he had Inez and her children murdered.

Pedro avenges his wife's death.

When Pedro became king, he tracked down his wife's murderers, had them brought back to Portugal and tortured them.

He ordered that Inez's body should be taken from her grave, dressed in coronation robes and crowned queen.

After the nobles had paid their humble respects to Inez's body, Pedro ordered her reburial.

A captive bride

In 1523 Turkish raiders captured a red-headed Russian girl. They called her Khurren, meaning "Laughing One", but she is better known as Roxelana. She was presented as a slave to the Sultan of Turkey Süleyman the Magnificent (1494-1566).

Sultan Süleyman

Süleyman and his men riding into battle in a scene from a 16th century miniature

Süleyman was captivated by Roxelana's wit and intelligence. He released her from slavery and married her, becoming the first sultan to marry in 600 years.

Roxelana's influence over the Sultan was so great that some courtiers even believed she was a witch. She was determined that her son, Selim, should be the next Sultan. By convincing Süleyman that Mustafa, heir to the throne, was plotting against him, she provoked the boy's execution. When Roxelana died in 1558, she knew that her son would inherit the Turkish empire.

Roxelana

In love with an older woman

Aged 11, Prince Henri (1519-59) who later became Henri II of France, fell in love with Diane de Poitièrs (1499-1566), a woman of 31. Although he was married in 1533 to Catherine de Medici, he pursued Diane until she agreed to be his mistress.

Henri and Diane remained deeply in love until Henri died of wounds accidentally inflicted during a tournament. His widow, Catherine de Medici, ordered Diane to return all the jewels that Henri had given her. Diane retired to the country until she died.

Diane de Poitièrs

The chosen one of the palace

Shah Jahan (1592-1666), one of the most powerful emperors of India, met his future wife while she was selling gifts in a bazaar. Their wedding was celebrated with a great procession and fireworks. The shah remained devoted to his wife for 19 years.

She was given the name Mumtaz Mahal which means "the Chosen One of the Palace". When she died in childbirth in 1631, he was griefstricken. He decided to build her a tomb of white marble, to match her beauty. He called it the Taj Mahal.

Mumtaz Mahal

Shah Jahan

Shah Jahan planned to build his own tomb of black marble, joined to the Taj Mahal by a silver bridge. But his plan was wrecked when in 1658 he was deposed by his son. Shah Jahan died in prison and was buried beside his wife's sarcophagus in an underground room in the Taj Mahal.

The Taj Mahal at Agra, India

The white marble of the Taj Mahal glows golden when the sun sets.

The Taj Mahal is hollow. It rests on a tower of bricks built above the ceiling of the tomb.

Sculptors carved hollows into the marble into which they slotted jewels.

The sarcophagi of Mumtaz Mahal and Shah Jahan.

Mumtaz is actually buried in an underground chamber.

Minarets

The tsar and tsarina

Martha Skavronskay (1684-1727), who later changed her name to Catherine, came from a peasant family in Lithuania. She worked for wealthy Russian families.

Tsar Peter of Russia (1672-1725) met Catherine and they quickly became close companions. They married in 1712 and had 12 children together.

The tsar changed the law so that Catherine could inherit the throne after he died.

Catherine I of Russia

A love story

♛ **A queen becomes king.** Experts think that when Pharaoh Akhenaten (14th century BC) realized that his wife Nefertiti could not give him a son, he married again. He tried to compensate Nefertiti by making her his co-ruler.

A bust of Nefertiti

♛ **Eleanor crosses.** When Eleanor of Castille (c.1245-90) died in Nottinghamshire, England, her husband Edward I of England (1239-1307) erected "Eleanor crosses" at every place her funeral procession stopped on its way to London.

Of 12 crosses, the Hardingstone is one of three that remain.

♛ **A divorced woman.** In 1937 Edward VIII of England gave up his throne to marry Mrs. Simpson. As king, and head of the Church of England, he was not allowed to marry a divorced woman.

Edward and Mrs. Simpson at their wedding in 1937

When kings and queens have complete control over the affairs of their countries, their decisions and judgement affect the lives of all their subjects. The consequences of a ruler afflicted by mental illness have often been catastrophic.

Caligula

Emperor Gaius of Rome (2- 41) was known as Caligula because of the little soldier's boots, known as *caligae*, that he wore as a child.

A coin showing a bust of Caligula

After only a few months in power, Caligula suffered from an illness which left him deranged. He soon began to act very strangely.

Examples of Caligula's strange actions

Caligula believed that he was a living god. He became very arrogant and would not listen to advice.

He made his horse, Incitatus, a government official and built a marble stable with an ivory manger for him.

Caligula married several women in quick succession, and even had an affair with his own sister.

Preoccupied with fears of plots and treason, Caligula murdered many prominent Roman citizens. His extravagance emptied Rome's treasury. Eventually, senators and members of his own bodyguard conspired against him, and Caligula was stabbed to death.

The king who was made of glass

During his reign, Charles VI of France (1368-1422) suffered periods of madness. One of his delusions was that he was made of glass and would break if touched.

He first fell ill in 1392. While he was recovering, the Constable of France was assassinated. Charles took a force of soldiers to punish the murderer. While passing through a forest, a man appeared and told the king to turn back. Charles was terrified, and he thought he was under attack. Lashing out with his sword, he killed several of his own men and then collapsed.

Charles slowly recovered his senses, but after tragedy struck at a palace ball (see picture below) he suffered another bout of madness.

France floundered without strong leadership, and suffered terrible defeat in foreign wars.

Charles VI of France

Charles VI was left emotionally disturbed after he and his friends caught fire at a ball.

Charles and his friends went to the ball dressed as savages.

A spark from a flaming torch ignited one of the costumes. Soon all six men were ablaze and three of them died from their injuries.

Charles was saved by a duchess who smothered the flames with her skirts.

A king who lived up to his name

Ivan IV (1530-84) became Tsar of Russia at the age of three. His mother and her lover acted as his regents. Caught up in a power struggle between the crown and Russian nobles, Ivan and his brother were badly treated and often lacked food and clothing.

Ivan grew up suspicious and cruel, earning his title "Ivan the Terrible". As a teenager he had a young nobleman named Prince Andrei Shuisky thrown to the palace dogs, which tore him to pieces.

Ivan had a vast cathedral built. But it is said that he blinded the two architects so that they could never build anything more magnificent.

The cathedral built by Ivan the Terrible in Moscow

This type of pointed roof is called a tent roof.

The cathedral is known as "St. Basil the Blessed", because Ivan's friend and adviser, Basil, is buried in it.

The proper name for the cathedral is the Cathedral of the Virgin of the Intercession by the Moat.

These domes were added in the 17th century. They are called "onion" domes, because of their shape.

The walls are made with brick and covered with blocks of stone.

The exterior of the cathedral was covered with bright tiling in the 17th century, giving it an oriental appearance.

The Cage

The Cage was introduced by Sultan Ahmet I of Turkey (1590-1617) as a method of avoiding wars of succession. When a new sultan came to the throne, all his brothers were locked up in a group of rooms known as the Cage. They were only released if they themselves were called upon to rule.

Many sultans emerged from the Cage completely insane.

When Osman II (1603-22) emerged from the Cage, he indulged his love of archery, using prisoners of war and his own servants as live targets.

Ibrahim the Mad, incarcerated for 22 years, had 280 of the ladies from his harem put in weighted sacks and drowned in the River Bosphorus.

One girl whose sack was not tied securely, swam to safety. When people heard her story, Ibrahim was deposed and murdered.

Ivan set up a special bodyguard called the *Oprichnina*, which tortured and killed his opponents. Ivan even took pleasure in assisting at many of the tortures and executions himself.

Ivan's savage temper was finally his downfall. In 1581, he argued with his eldest son. In a rage Ivan attacked him viciously and the prince died of his injuries. Ivan ended his life an embittered old man, leaving his throne to his second son Fedor, a sickly and incapable young man.

A woodcut showing Ivan the Terrible

The Swan king

When Ludwig II (1845-86) became King of Bavaria his subjects thought him a handsome, capable leader. In reality, he was a sad and lonely young man. Increasingly detached from reality, he became obsessed with legends and fairy tales, particularly the story of the Swan King.

Ludwig's passion for building (see page 17) and for the composer

This life-size swan vase was kept in Ludwig's bathroom.

Wagner (see page 19) drove Bavaria to bankruptcy. His ministers had him removed from office, declared him insane and imprisoned him in Berg Castle.

On June 12, 1886, the king and his doctor went walking in the castle grounds. When they did not return, a search party was organized. Both men were found drowned in the lake. Nobody knows if Ludwig's death was suicide or an accident. An examination found no water in his lungs, which would suggest that he did not drown.

Ludwig of Bavaria

Rational rulers?

♚ **Fire! Fire!** Emperor Nero of Rome (37-68) had his mother, his wife and many senators murdered. Some people believe that he started the fire which destroyed two thirds of Rome.

A statue of Nero

♛ **Juana the mad.** Juana (1479-1555), heiress to the Spanish throne, refused to allow her dead husband to be buried. Declared unfit to govern, she was locked up for 50 years, until her death.

Juana, known as "la loca" meaning "the mad"

♚ **The king is mad.** George III of England (1738-1820) suffered from periods of insanity. He foamed at the mouth, talked incessantly and he even thought an oak tree was Frederick of Prussia. Doctors now suggest that the king had porphyria, a disease which affects the brain.

George III of England

In the past, if a scandal occurred in royal circles it was covered up quickly and efficiently. Some events were so well disguised that historians still cannot penetrate the mystery that surrounds them.

Princes in the Tower

In 1674 the skeletons of two boys were found in the Tower of London. Historians believe that they could have belonged to King Edward V of England (1470-83), and his brother Richard, Duke of York.

After only two months on the throne Edward and Richard were imprisoned by their uncle, who became Richard III. The princes disappeared mysteriously. Nobody knows exactly what happened. They may have been murdered, but Edward was ill while staying in the Tower and could have died of natural causes. His brother might have been smuggled abroad.

The princes as painted by Millais (1829-96)

This plan shows the Tower of London as it was when the bones were found.

Murder at the Kirk o'Field

Soon after marrying her cousin Lord Darnley, Mary, Queen of Scots (1542-87) found that she had made a mistake. Darnley was a cruel man. He and his friends brutally murdered Mary's secretary, David Rizzio, in front of her.

Lord Darnley

When Darnley fell ill in 1567, Mary took him to a mansion in Edinburgh called the Kirk o'Field. She visited him every day, and sat for hours reading by his bedside.

On the evening of February 9, the queen left her husband's room to attend a wedding celebration. At 2:00am the house in which Darnley slept was blown to pieces by gunpowder. His body was found in the garden. However, he had not been killed by the explosion. He had been strangled.

Three months later, Mary married the Earl of Bothwell, who is thought to have arranged Darnley's murder. Letters from Mary to Bothwell found in a casket proved that she knew of the plot in advance. Mary, however, insisted that the letters were all forgeries.

Mary Queen of Scots

A contemporary sketch of Darnley's murder at Kirk o'Field

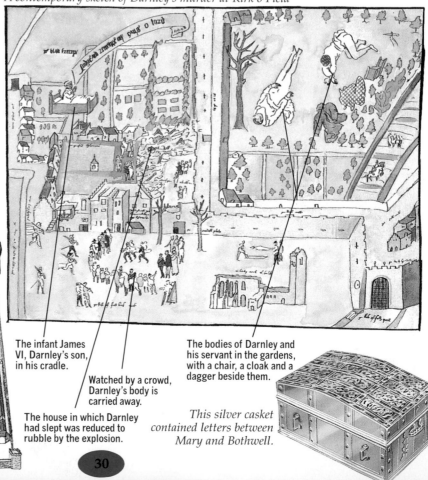

The infant James VI, Darnley's son, in his cradle.

Watched by a crowd, Darnley's body is carried away.

The house in which Darnley had slept was reduced to rubble by the explosion.

The bodies of Darnley and his servant in the gardens, with a chair, a cloak and a dagger beside them.

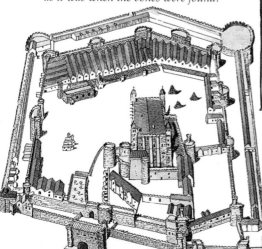

This silver casket contained letters between Mary and Bothwell.

Witchcraft at the French court

In 1667, the Chief of Police in Paris discovered that witchcraft was rife in the city. Courtiers were involved in devil worship, sacrifices, poisons and love potions.

Athénais de Montespan, (1641-1707) the lover of Louis XIV, was said to have visited a witch and used black magic to seduce the king. 36 people were arrested. Louis ended his affair with Athénais. Fearing a scandal, he closed the police's investigation and destroyed the evidence.

This contemporary picture shows the trial of one of the suspected witches.

The death of a valet

In 1810, palace officials released a report of an attempt on the life of the Duke of Cumberland, the son of George III of England.

The duke's version of events that night

At 2:30am on May 31, the duke was attacked by his valet, Joseph Sellis, wielding a sword. The duke was badly wounded.

The duke called for help and managed to stagger into a room where Neale, one of his attendants, was sleeping.

After the attack, Sellis ran off to his own room, where he was later discovered dead. His throat had been cut.

A verdict of suicide was delivered at Sellis's inquest, despite several inconsistencies. First, the wound on the valet's throat was too deep to have been self-inflicted. Second, the cut was made by a right-handed person; Sellis was left-handed.

Many people thought that the duke himself had killed Sellis, but his own wounds were so severe that this is almost impossible. The truth remains a mystery.

Arsenic on St. Helena

The French emperor Napoleon (see page 35) died a prisoner on the island of St. Helena off the west coast of Africa. His death certificate says that he died of cancer, but the seven doctors who examined his body could not agree on the cause of death.

In the 1950s a Swedish dentist named Dr. Forshufvud, declared that Napoleon had been poisoned. While on St. Helena, the emperor had sent locks of his hair to people as souvenirs. Examining strands of this hair, Forshufvud found high levels of arsenic, a deadly poison.

This series of portraits of Napoleon show him getting increasingly fat, which supports the theory that he was poisoned.

1815

1817

1819

1820

The doctor suggested that Count Charles-Tristan de Montholon, stationed on the island, had stolen a large sum of money from the French army. Facing ruin and imprisonment if prosecuted, the Count may have accepted a pardon in return for poisoning Napoleon.

♛ **Poison at the palace.** During World War II, King Boris III of Bulgaria would not support Hitler, the German leader. After visiting Hitler, Boris fell ill and died in great pain. Was he poisoned? After the war Boris's coffin vanished mysteriously.

Adolf Hitler

Tragedy at Mayerling

On January 30, 1889 the bodies of Prince Rudolph, heir to the Austro-Hungarian Empire, and his lover Mary Vetsera were found in a royal hunting lodge at Mayerling. Revelations of a suicide pact between the lovers would have caused a scandal, so every effort was made to cover up what had happened that night.

The prince was buried with full ceremony, but Mary's body was dressed, propped up in a coach, and taken by her uncles to be buried in secret. Her mother was sent to Venice, to announce that Mary had died there.

Prince Rudolph's funeral procession outside the hunting lodge at Mayerling

Rudolph's coffin on a horse-drawn carriage

If a monarch dies leaving a child to inherit the throne, a person called a regent is appointed to run the kingdom. The regent remains in power until the child is old enough to rule. Some monarchs are best remembered for the events of their childhood, while there are regents who are more renowned than the monarchs they represented.

A gift for a young king

Pepi II (c.2262-2162BC) ruled Egypt from the age of six until he died aged 100, a record-breaking 94 years. There are many stories of the life of the child pharaoh. Once, a nobleman called Harkhuf sent news to Pepi that he had a "dancing dwarf" as a gift for the king. Historians think that on a trade expedition, Harkhuf had found a pygmy from West Africa.

Pepi wrote to Harkhuf giving him strict instructions to look after the pygmy carefully. Harkhuf was so proud of the letter that he had it recorded on the walls of his tomb.

An alabaster statue of King Pepi on his mother's knee

Because he is a king, the child is depicted as a miniature adult.

An ambitious stepmother

In c.1503BC, Queen Hatshepsut (1540-1481BC) became regent for her stepson, Tuthmosis III (see page 12). Within two years she seized power during a ceremony in a temple.

How Hatshepsut seized power

As a statue of a god was carried past Hatshepsut, it became so heavy that the priests carrying it sank to their knees.

Declaring this was a sign that the gods wanted her to rule, Hatshepsut pronounced herself "King" of Egypt.

She ruled well for 20 years, and is believed to have led successful military campaigns in Nubia and Syria.

After Hatshepsut died, her successor Tuthmosis III came to power. He could not bear to be reminded of the stepmother who had dominated him so completely. He gave orders for all her statues and inscriptions to be destroyed.

Archaeologists have only recently begun piecing together the surviving fragments of stone, in order to learn about Hatshepsut's great military achievements.

A statue of Hatshepsut, shown in men's clothing

Emperor Sheng Shen

Emperor Tai-tsung of China had many lovers, but preferred a woman called Wu Ze Tian (623-705). But Wu realized that the emperor would never marry her, so she married his son, who later became emperor. When her husband died, Wu acted as regent for one of her sons. But by 690, she was no longer content to be the power behind the throne. Wu gave herself the title Emperor Sheng Shen and seized the throne. Once in a position of power, she gave orders for many of the people who had opposed her to be tracked down and killed.

This figure shows the costume women wore at court.

After an incredible 55 years in power, Wu was finally deposed during a coup led by her eldest son.

A fine example

A more virtuous queen mother was Blanche of Castille (1188-1252) who became regent for her son Louis IX of France in 1226. She ruled France very successfully.

Blanche also managed to raise her family well. Louis became one of France's most respected kings. He asked his mother's advice for the rest of her life. When he left France to go on Crusades (see page 23), Blanche ruled in his absence.

Louis IX leaves for a Crusade

An unusual coronation

Henry III of England (1207-72) became king at the age of nine. Because his father had lost the real crown while crossing a muddy river, he was crowned with a chaplet (a kind of necklace) which belonged to his mother, Isabella.

This painting shows Henry being crowned at Gloucester Cathedral.

When Queen Isabella decided to return to her native France to remarry, a former warrior and loyal member of court named William Marshall was chosen to act as regent to the young king. Marshall, and the regents who succeeded him, ruled the country sensibly until Henry was old enough to govern himself.

A medieval picture showing William Marshall's formidable battle skills.

The last Chinese emperor

Leaders of the Chinese Revolution forced the emperor, Pu Yi (1906-67), to abdicate his throne when he was only four years old. The emperor continued to live in the Forbidden City (see page 6) until 1924, when he was forced to leave.

The communists who controlled China forced Pu Yi to live as an ordinary citizen and gave him the name Henry Pu Yi. He was imprisoned for 5 years and after his release he worked as a gardener and a librarian.

Pu Yi as a young child.

The Forbidden City, where Pu Yi lived until he was 18.

(see page 6)

Sons and mothers

♛**Respect.** In the kingdom of Benin, Africa, queen mothers continued to wield considerable power after their children were adults and ready to rule themselves.

The carved head of a queen mother of Benin

♛**Permission granted.** Alice Botiller, nurse to Henry VI of England (1421-71), made the young king sign a charter which permitted her to scold him without fear of being punished.

The coat of arms of Henry VI of England

♛**Royal prisoner.** Louis (1785-95), heir to the throne of France, was thrown into prison after the execution of his parents, Louis XVI and Marie Antoinette (see page 21). Brutal treatment resulted in his death when he was only 10 years old.

(see page 21)

The Emperor's Dragon Throne stands within the Hall of Supreme Harmony.

The Hall of Supreme Harmony was raised on a three-tiered terrace

A curved canal, called "Golden Stream"

A drum and bell were sounded whenever the emperor passed through the Meridian Gate, the Forbidden City's main entrance.

Many monarchs have occupied thrones to which they have little or no claim. The routes they have taken vary from marriage to conquest, rebellion, or election. Some "self-made" kings and queens have managed to pass their titles on to their children, while others have only remained in power for a short time.

Pepin the Short

In the 8th century, King Chilperic II ruled the Frankish empire, which covered much of central and eastern Europe. In 751, backed by a group of powerful nobles, Pepin the Short (c.715-68) deposed Chilperic II. He cut off Chilperic's hair and had him taken to live in a monastery. The Pope confirmed Pepin's succession to the throne, and went to France to carry out the coronation himself.

Pepin ruled bravely and well. The throne was inherited by his son Charlemagne who became one of the most powerful rulers of his time (see page 19).

Pepin the Short

Robert Bruce

When the direct line of the Scottish royal family died out in 1290, there were 13 people with a claim to the throne. Among them was Robert Bruce (1274-1329), who was determined to secure the throne for himself. It is even said that Bruce stabbed a man named John Comyn, who was one of his 13 rivals for the throne.

A picture of Robert Bruce

Edward I of England saw the disputes over the Scottish throne as an opportunity to claim control of Scotland. Bruce was crowned King of Scotland in 1306, but he subsequently suffered two military defeats at the hands of Edward. In 1314, at the Battle of Bannockburn, Bruce returned to face and defeat an English army twice the size of his own. He ruled Scotland until he died of leprosy in 1329.

The seal of Robert Bruce

How to steal a throne

At the age of 16, Princess Sophia of Anhalt-Zerbst (1729-96) married Grand Duke Peter, heir to the Russian throne. She changed her name to Catherine. The marriage had been arranged by her mother, but it was not a happy one.

Peter became tsar in 1762, but he was neither a strong nor an efficient leader.

A brooch showing Catherine

Catherine and her lover, Gregory Orlov, joined the Russian army in a revolt against Peter.

The tsar was dethroned and murdered. Catherine became tsarina and was so successful that she earned herself the title "Catherine the Great". Her son Paul inherited the throne when she died.

A portrait of Catherine the Great

William conquers England

Edward of England (1003-66) promised his throne to William, Duke of Normandy (1027-87). But after Edward's death this promise was broken, so William decided to seize the crown for himself by force. The story of his invasion of England was recorded in the Bayeux Tapestry, a strip of tapestry.

William of Normandy who became King of England

These extracts from the tapestry show William's quest for the crown.

Harold Godwinsson, Earl of Wessex, was forced to stay at William's court in Normandy, after being shipwrecked. William forced Harold to swear to support his claim to the English throne.

Harold made the promise, but he did not realize that holy relics were hidden beneath the altar on which he had sworn. This made his promise a sacred oath.

A do-it-yourself emperor

During the French Revolution the king and queen were executed (see page 21). Following the revolution, France was thrown into a state of chaos. Napoleon Bonaparte (1769-1821), a brilliant general in the French army, saw an opportunity to seize power.

In 1799, he marched into the parliament building and dismissed its members. He set up a new government, called the Consulate. Declaring himself the First Consul, he became the French leader.

Napoleon was not satisfied as First Consul. In 1804 he had himself elected Emperor of France. In an elaborate ceremony at the Cathedral of Nôtre Dame, Paris, Napoleon took the imperial diadem from Pope Pius VII and placed it on his own head.

The imperial diadem

This painting, by the artist Jacques Louis David, shows the coronation of Napoleon.

Napoleon's mother

Napoleon, wearing the imperial diadem, crowns his wife.

Pope Pius VII

Napoleon's first wife, Josephine

Seizing power

Elected king. In 987 Hugh Capet (c.938-996) was elected King of France, by fellow noblemen, in place of the incompetent kings who had been in power before.

The coronation of Hugh Capet

To the death. When the King of Siam died in 1424, his two eldest sons decided to fight each other for the throne.

They fought on elephants, but both died, and their younger brother became king.

A slave king. In 1790, black slaves on the island of Haiti, in the Caribbean, revolted against their French rulers. Their leader, Toussaint L'Ouverture (1746-1803) was betrayed by the rebels, but one of his followers became Emperor of Haiti.

Toussaint l'Ouverture

When King Edward died in 1066, Harold broke his oath and accepted the crown. This gave William the excuse to invade England.

With a fleet of 700 ships, and an estimated 10,000 men, William attacked England later that year. His army was victorious at the Battle of Hastings.

In battle, Harold was killed, either by an arrow that pierced his eye or by a rider with a sword. William was crowned King of England.

Throughout history, monarchs have been challenged by people called pretenders, who claim that they themselves should be on the throne. Many pretenders were impostors, lured by the promise of great power and wealth. Others were provoked by the ambitious enemies of reigning monarchs. But a few pretenders may indeed have had an honest claim to the throne.

The changeling king

Shortly after the death of King Louis X of France in 1316, his wife gave birth to a son and heir, John I of France. However, the new baby king died when he was only a few days old, and was succeeded by his uncle, Philip. Stories began to spread that the baby king John had in fact been murdered by Philip's mother-in-law, an ambitious woman who wanted her daughter to become Queen of France.

In 1354, a merchant named Giovanni (the Italian version of the name John) from Sienna, Italy, was told an extraordinary tale, which suggested these stories might have been true.

The confession of Giovanni's mother

On her death bed, Giovanni's French mother confessed to him that he was not her son, but John I, the rightful King of France.

She told him that she had been the baby king's nurse. Fearing an attack on him, she placed her own baby son in the royal cradle.

The baby who had died in 1316 was her own son, but she had kept her secret and raised the king herself.

Many of the citizens of Sienna supported Giovanni's story, as did the King of Hungary. But the ruler of Naples refused to believe the story and threw Giovanni in jail, where he died in 1362. Even today nobody knows if Giovanni's dying mother was telling the truth.

Lambert Simnel

King Henry VII (1457-1509), had a rather weak claim to the English throne. This was exploited by his enemies. In 1487, they persuaded a young pretender named Lambert Simnel (c.1477-c.1534) to challenge Henry. Simnel said that he was Edward, the Earl of Warwick, the son of one of Richard III's brothers.

The Earl of Warwick had been reported dead. In fact he was a prisoner in the Tower of London, where he had been since his childhood. To prove that Simnel's claims were false, Henry paraded Warwick through the streets of London.

A portrait of Henry VII

Lambert Simnel was captured and punished. It was unusual for a pretender to survive at all, but he was sent to work in the royal kitchens, where he lived until the age of 57.

A prince returns from the grave

A more serious threat to Henry VII's throne was a young man who claimed to be Richard, Duke of York. Richard was the younger of the two princes in the Tower of London. He said that he had been rescued from the Tower and smuggled out of England. He was brought up under the name Perkin Warbeck in Flanders, an area of Europe now part of France.

Warbeck raised a small army and invaded England in 1498, but he soon faced defeat. Surrendering in return for a royal pardon, he was imprisoned in the Tower. After trying to escape and raise another rebellion, he was executed in 1499.

If Warbeck was an impostor, he was a very convincing one. He bore a striking resemblance to Edward IV, father of the princes.

A view of the Tower of London as it would have looked in the 16th century.

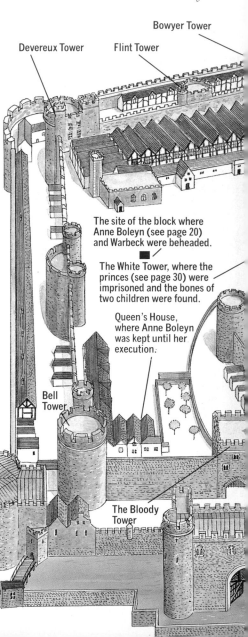

Bowyer Tower

Devereux Tower   Flint Tower

The site of the block where Anne Boleyn (see page 20) and Warbeck were beheaded.

The White Tower, where the princes (see page 30) were imprisoned and the bones of two children were found.

Queen's House, where Anne Boleyn was kept until her execution.

Bell Tower

The Bloody Tower

Margaret, Duchess of Burgundy was the sister of Edward IV, and the aunt of the two princes. She believed that Warbeck really was her nephew. Some historians think he may have been one of Edward IV's illegitimate sons. But with the deep mystery that surrounded the fate of the two young princes, it is just possible that Warbeck was telling the truth.

Edward IV

Brick Tower

Martin Tower

Brass Mount

Constable Tower

Broad Arrow Tower

Salt Tower

Lanthorn Tower

The Queen's Gallery

Jewel House (see page 5)

The Privy Garden

The moat

Prisoners, like Warbeck, were brought through Traitors' Gate.

The False Dimitri

In 1584, Ivan IV of Russia (see page 28) died and was succeeded by his son Fedor. Fedor was a weak leader and Russia was really controlled by a man named Godunov. When Fedor died, Godunov became tsar.

Godunov's royal seal

Ivan's youngest son, Dimitri (1583-91), the next heir to the throne, died at the age of nine in a bizarre accident involving a knife. Some people began to suspect that Godunov had murdered him; others thought he was still alive.

In 1603, Grigoriy Otrepieff, a monk, claimed that he was Dimitri. The False Dimitri, as he is known, invaded Russia and was crowned tsar, but soon became unpopular and was murdered in a revolt.

A second pretender appeared, also claiming to be Dimitri, but he did not look at all like his predecessor. He too was soon murdered.

Tsarevich Dimitri

Grigoriy Otrepieff

The last of the Romanovs

Most historians believe that Anastasia, daughter of Tsar Nicholas II of Russia, was executed with her family (see page 21). But the bones of two of the Romanov children have never been discovered.

In 1920 a young woman appeared in Berlin claiming to be Anastasia. She took the name Anna Anderson and spent 50 years trying to prove her royal identity. Many relatives of the Romanovs rejected her claims. Others believed her, because she knew detailed information about Anastasia and life at court.

After her death at the age of 82, Anna's true identity remained a mystery. But in 1994, tests on her body tissue showed that she could not have been the tsar's daughter.

The room in which the Romanovs were shot and (inset) Anna Anderson

Great pretenders

♛ **The Bonnie Pretender.** In 1745 Bonnie Prince Charlie invaded England, claiming the throne as the grandson of James II of Britain. When his army was defeated, a young woman called Flora MacDonald helped him escape to France by disguising him as a maid named Betty Burke .

Bonnie Prince Charlie

♛ **An unlikely story.** Louis XVII of France died in prison in 1795, but several people claimed to be him, including a watchmaker, and a man who was half Indian.

Many people have achieved great power and influence by becoming the trusted and valued friend of a monarch. But the sudden loss of royal friendship has often had disastrous or even fatal consequences.

A monument to friendship

Amenhotep, son of Hapu, was a talented official who rapidly rose through the ranks in the service of Amenhotep III of Egypt (c.1411-1375BC). The pharaoh paid many tributes to his chief minister, and he even put up statues of him in the temple of Karnak. When people came to the temple to pray to their god-king, they had to address the statue of his minister first, just as they had to do in matters of government. When minister Amenhotep died, his tomb was built in a style normally reserved for an Egyptian king. The Egyptian

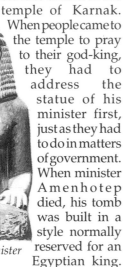

A statue of minister Amenhotep

people worshipped him as a god of wisdom for several generations after his death.

Plotting against the emperor

Roman emperor Tiberius (42BC-37) lived in constant fear of assassination. The only man he trusted was his friend Sejanus. Sejanus was a commander in the Praetorian Guard, which was the emperor's bodyguard.

Sejanus took advantage of Tiberius's fears. He managed to persuade the emperor to move to the island of Capri, convincing him he would be safe from assassins.

The uniform of a Praetorian guardsman

A helmet made of iron

A leather tunic with metal strips attached to it allowed freedom of movement.

A dagger hung from the left of the soldier's belt.

A groin-guard made of leather and metal.

A shield made of wood and leather with a metal rim. It was about 1.20m (4ft) by 0.7m (2.3ft), and curved.

Heavy sandals with metal studs

In this way Sejanus made sure that he was the only link of communication between Rome and the emperor.

Left in charge of Rome, Sejanus became increasingly powerful. Anyone who disagreed with him was executed or forced to commit suicide. Many of Tiberius's relatives were among Sejanus's victims.

Eventually Sejanus grew too ambitious for his own good. He devised a plan to marry Tiberius's niece, Livilla. Together they plotted to murder Tiberius and seize the throne. But Tiberius was warned of their scheme and Sejanus was executed.

A bust of Emperor Tiberius

Words spoken in anger

Thomas Becket (1118-70) was a close friend of Henry II of England (1133-89). The king made him Archbishop of Canterbury, expecting his support. But Becket took his role as a servant of the church very seriously, and soon the friends argued bitterly. They disagreed over whether churchmen should be tried in a royal court, or in a separate church court.

In a rage, Henry declared that he wanted to be rid of Thomas Becket. Overhearing these words, four knights rode to Canterbury Cathedral and killed Becket.

The murder of Becket as shown in a 15th-century illustration

Becket is shown with a halo as he was made a saint in 1173.

The knights are dressed in chain mail with tunics depicting their coats of arms.

The knights were named Reginald Fitzurse, Hugh de Merville, William de Tracy and Richard le Breton.

Friends and enemies

Queen Anne of England (1665-1714) was very fond of Sarah Jennings (1660-1722) her lady-in-waiting (a personal attendant). They had been friends since childhood. Anne even allowed Sarah to call her Mrs Morley so that the difference in their ranks would be forgotten.

Sarah's duties as lady-in-waiting and mistress of the robes

Sarah oversaw the ladies who dressed the queen, and kept a list of all the clothes in the royal wardrobe.

Sarah's main role was as companion to the queen. Here they are playing cards together.

Sarah ensured that all the queen's robes were clean and repaired, and ordered new materials if necessary.

Sarah's influence with the queen ensured the political success of her husband, the Duke of Marlborough, and his allies.

Sarah's position was a precarious one. Her fiery temper led her and Anne to quarrel. Anne transferred her friendship to a quieter lady-in-waiting named Abigail Marsham, Sarah's cousin. Sarah was dismissed from court and went abroad.

La Pompadour

Jeanne Poisson (1721-64) was determined to become the lover of Louis XV of France (1710-74). She came from a middle class background, which made it difficult to meet the king. But she caught his eye when she went to watch him hunt. Captivated by her beauty, Louis XV brought Jeanne to live at the palace at Versailles, where she became his "reigning mistress". He gave her the title Marquise de Pompadour.

Louis XV

La Pompadour, as she became known, dominated the French court for 20 years. She remained Louis' close friend until her death.

Jeanne's style of dress became very fashionable at court

Her hair was rolled back from her forehead and decorated. Later, this style became very exaggerated (see page 8).

Whalebones and canes were used to make her waist look tiny.

An opening in the front of the skirt showed a decorated petticoat.

The frilly sleeves of her under-dress

Buckled shoes

The mad monk

Tsar Nicholas II of Russia (1868-1918) discovered that his son and heir, Alexi, had a dangerous disease which prevented his blood from clotting. A tiny scratch could result in a sufferer bleeding to death.

Rasputin (c.1871-1916), a monk and healer, had a mysterious ability to reduce Alexi's suffering. He became a close friend of the tsar, advising him on policies, and choosing his ministers. Many people resented the monk's power and influence. In 1916 a group of nobles gave Rasputin cyanide, shot him and pushed his body under the ice of the frozen River Neva.

A cartoon showing Rasputin at court

Friends in high places

👑 **Best friends.** Hugh le Despenser, friend of Edward II of England (1284-1327), was executed when the king was overthrown. Lady Diana Spencer, who is now the Princess of Wales, is his direct descendant.

Edward II of England

👑 **An unlikely pair.** Queen Victoria and her servant, John Brown, remained close friends for 20 years. The queen allowed him to bully and protect her. When Brown died, Victoria erected memorials to him in many of her royal residences.

Many monarchs have had spectacular funerals and great monuments have been raised to preserve their memory. In many cultures, people believed that dead rulers would need riches and servants after death. Monarchs were often buried with all kinds of gifts and provisions for the next life.

Sumerian burials

In the 1920s, Sir Leonard Woolley, an archaeologist, uncovered tombs which dated from between c.2650-2500BC. They belonged to the rulers of the city of Ur in Mesopotamia (now part of Iraq). Each tomb included a chamber containing the royal body. Outside the chamber lay courtiers, guards and servants who had taken poison and died to be with their rulers.

The tomb of Queen Shudu-ad of Ur

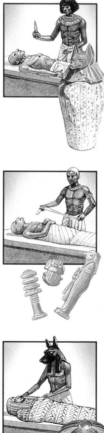

Stone tomb chamber

Antechamber

Queen Shudu-ad

Gold, silver and copper bowls and a box inlaid with shell and lapis lazuli.

Wooden chest

Bowls

Gaming board

Wooden sledge

Five soldiers on guard

Two oxen to pull the sledge, and four grooms.

Ten handmaidens wearing headdresses and gold and silver trinkets.

Burying the pharaohs of Egypt

The Egyptians believed it was important to preserve a person's body for the next life. They preserved the bodies of dead pharaohs in a process called mummification (see below).

Once mummified, the rulers of the Old Kingdom (c.2649-2150BC) were buried in huge stone pyramids (see page 16), with piles of treasure for the next life. But robbers managed to plunder the tombs, so the bodies of later pharaohs were placed in chambers cut into cliffs near Luxor, where soldiers could guard them.

Mummifying a pharaoh's body

The embalmer made a cut in the left side of the body. He removed the organs and stored them in containers known as canopic jars.

A canopic jar containing organs

Salt called *natron* was packed around the body to dry it out. The insides were filled with linen or sawdust, resin and salt. Then the body was wrapped in bandages.

Jewels and lucky charms were placed between the layers of bandages.

The chief embalmer placed a portrait mask over the mummy's face. It was then put in a coffin.

The portrait mask was thought to enable the spirit to recognize its body.

Tutankhamun's tomb

The tomb of 18 year-old King Tutankhamun (14th century BC) lay undiscovered for 30 centuries. In 1922, men working for Howard Carter, an archaeologist, found steps leading to the door of the young king's tomb. It had been covered by rocks when the tomb of Ramesses VI was built.

Carter opening the tomb of Tutankhamun

Carter made a hole in the door of the tomb and peered inside. When he was asked if he could see anything, he said "Yes, wonderful things." Inside were the riches of a royal Egyptian burial, the only pharaoh's treasure ever to be recovered unplundered by robbers.

The four coffins of Tutankhamun

The funeral mask is a portrait of the young king.

This coffin is made of solid gold.

Mummified body

China's terracotta army

In 1974, farmers digging a well in Xian, China, found a huge underground complex. It was the tomb of Emperor Shih Huang Ti (see page 17), the largest tomb ever discovered. The burial chamber lies beneath modern villages and factories, making excavation work very slow. Ancient records say the tomb is protected by traps, such as crossbows set up to kill anyone who enters.

Outside the burial chamber, archaeologists have begun to uncover an army of 7500 pottery soldiers, horses and chariots. They had been put there to fight for the emperor in his next life.

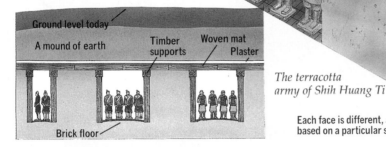

A kneeling terracotta crossbow man

All the figures are life-sized.

Originally they were brightly painted.

A squad of spear men

Four life-sized horses pulled each chariot

The terracotta army of Shih Huang Ti

Each face is different, based on a particular soldier.

A cross section of the pits in which the soldiers and horses stood

Ground level today

A mound of earth

Timber supports

Woven mat
Plaster

Brick floor

The outer coffins are made of wood covered with 22 carat gold and semi precious stones.

Burying a great queen

Queen Elizabeth I of England (1533-1603) died on March 24, 1603, at the age of 70. Her body was buried in Westminster Abbey a month later.

At Elizabeth's funeral, her coffin rested on a chariot pulled by four white horses. A wax effigy of the queen, clothed in royal robes, lay on top. The chariot was protected by a canopy carried by six knights.

This picture of Elizabeth's funeral procession was painted at the time of her death.

A wax effigy of Queen Elizabeth

Knights

The horse-drawn carriage was followed by a procession of mourners.

Fit for a king

👑 **Resting place.** The tomb of King Mausolus of Halicarnassus (now part of Turkey) was one of the most magnificent ever built. From his name comes the word mausoleum, meaning a building containing tombs.

During the 20th century, many monarchies have been overthrown, and the power of others has been restricted. But some countries are still ruled by powerful kings and queens.

Dictators and military leaders

Some monarchies have been destroyed in times of violence and revolution. The rulers that have replaced them have often ruled as strictly as any sovereign.

Mao Tse-tung (1893-1976) was the leader of the communists in China. He came to power after the years of unrest that followed the fall of the last Emperor of China (see page 33). He wielded great power over the country. His political ideas were written down in the "Little Red Book", which had to be carried by every citizen.

A picture of Mao Tse-tung

Mao Tse-tung was treated with great reverence. People were not allowed to throw away his picture. As newspapers were full of portraits of Mao, people saved every copy. Soon families had to move out of their houses which were full of newspapers. It was an offence to sit on a pile of newspapers containing Mao's picture.

Stamps commemorating China becoming a republic in 1949.

Presidents and heads of state

In some countries a monarch has been replaced by a leader elected by the people. These countries are called republics, and the title given to the leader is head of state or president. Many presidents are surrounded with the pomp and grandeur often associated with royalty and queens. For example, John F. Kennedy (1917-63) was one of the most popular presidents of the United States. He and his wife Jackie were seen by many people to be the ideal American family. During Kennedy's time in office the White House (the American presidential residence) was known as Camelot, after the court of the legendary King Arthur (see page 45).

The seal of the President of the United States of America

On November 22, 1963, John Kennedy was assassinated in Dallas, Texas. The event shocked the whole world.

President Kennedy and his wife Jackie, moments before he was shot and killed.

Constitutional monarchs

As countries have adopted democratic government (rule by the people), so the powers of monarchs have diminished. Today many kings and queens have little say in the running of their countries. They exist alongside governments that hold political power.

In many countries, royal power has been limited by a constitution. This is a set of guidelines outlining the powers and political principles according to which a country is governed.

Belgium, Sweden and the United Kingdom, whose flags are shown here, have constitutional monarchies.

A modern monarch

Elizabeth II, Queen of Great Britain and Northern Ireland is a modern, constitutional monarch. She has no role in governing the country. All political issues are decided by an institution which is called Parliament.

As queen, she is given information and advice on political issues by representatives of the government. But she has to remain free from ties to any political party.

Queen Elizabeth II's coat of arms

When laws have been passed by Parliament the queen gives them royal assent with the words "La reine le veut". This means it is the queen's wish that they become law.

Royal Duties

As a modern monarch, Queen Elizabeth II has a wide selection of duties to perform. She must lead formal ceremonies, such as the opening of Parliament. She is also head of the armed forces, and all soldiers have to swear loyalty to her.

Members of the royal family often visit foreign countries. This helps to maintain friendly relations between Great Britain and other nations, and encourages trade. The queen also supports many charities, using her name and influence to help them to raise money.

The queen can reward people whose actions have benefited the country. One of the top awards is a knighthood. The queen knights a person by touching them on their shoulders with a sword. This is called "dubbing".

Queen Elizabeth II travels by carriage to the official opening of Parliament.

Elizabeth II meets Jamaican women on a state visit.

Her Majesty Queen Elizabeth II, a state portrait by Sir James Gunn, painted in 1953

Still powerful

Today, there are a number of countries where the monarchs have retained substantial powers. For example, the leadership of King Fahd Ibn Abdulaziz (b.1921), who inherited the throne of Saudi Arabia in 1982, is of central importance to his kingdom.

King Fahd Ibn Abdulaziz

As head of Saudi Arabia's government as well as king, Fahd's decisions dictate policies both at home and in foreign affairs.

Return of the monarchy

There are some countries in which monarchies have been returned to power. In 1931, King Alfonso XIII of Spain was forced to leave the country when his subjects voted for Spain to become a republic. Later, Spain was ruled by Francisco Franco, a military dictator, who decided that the monarchy should be restored after his death. He named as his successor Alfonso's grandson, Juan Carlos, who became king in 1975.

A stamp showing King Juan Carlos

Teenager Grand Duke Georgy is the heir to the throne of Russia. He is a relative of Tsar Nicholas

Grand Duke Georgy

II of Russia, who was deposed by revolution in 1918 (see page 21).

Grand Duke Georgy has recently been granted Russian citizenship, and will receive his education at a Russian naval academy that was founded by his ancestor, Tsar Peter the Great. Maybe one day the Russian royal family will be restored as a constitutional monarchy.

Modern monarchs

⚜ **Divine ancestors.** Despite being a modern monarch, Elizabeth II can, in theory, trace her family tree back to Woden, an ancient father-god of Europe. She is descended from an Anglo-Saxon king named Cedric, who claimed to trace his family back to Woden.

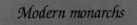
Woden, or Odin as he is called in Scandinavia.

Before writing was widely used, stories of kings and queens were passed on by word of mouth. Often, as time passed, these stories were distorted and became extravagant tales of mythical figures. Historians often try to find out the facts which inspired the myths.

Gilgamesh

Legend tells of Gilgamesh, a king of Sumer (now Iraq), who set out on a quest looking for eternal life.

Gilgamesh's quest for eternal life

Gilgamesh went to the land of Dilmun. He met a man named Ut-napishtim, who told him that the secret of eternal life was a magic herb.

After many dangers, Gilgamesh found the herb, but it was eaten by a snake while he slept, depriving him of his goal.

Historians have found a king called Gilgamesh of Uruk, on an ancient list of Sumerian kings. The land of Dilmun has been identified as the island of Bahrain.

Amazon Queen

Hippolyte was the Queen of the Amazons, a band of women warriors described in Greek legends.

Amazons fighting Hercules

The Ancient Greeks believed that the Amazons lived on the coast of the Black Sea, in what is now Turkey. Later, they are said to have moved north, marrying Scythian horsemen. Their descendants were a people called the Sarmatians.

A statue of a Scythian archer

In the 1950s, archaeologists began to find graves of Sarmatian women containing weapons. This suggests the Amazons were not entirely mythical.

The palace at Knossos

According to Greek legend, the god Zeus fell in love with a princess called Europa. Assuming the shape of a bull, he swam to Crete with her on his back.

A picture of Europa and Zeus from an ancient vase

One of Europa's sons, Minos, became the King of Crete and lived in the palace of Knossos. Historians think that Minos was a title given to all the rulers of Crete, rather than one particular king.

Another legend tells of a Greek prince called Theseus who visited Crete. He killed a terrible monster, half human and half bull. It was called the Minotaur and lived in a maze called the Labyrinth.

To later generations, the ruins of Knossos may well have seemed like a maze, with its many rooms and corridors. The story of the Minotaur may have been inspired by a Cretan king wearing a bull's head mask during religious rituals.

This picture shows the palace of Knossos and some of its most famous artefacts.

This wall painting shows a young man in an elaborate headdress which suggests that he was a prince or a king.

Many bright wall paintings (like the one shown above) decorated the royal apartments

The palace was built and rebuilt several times between c.1900BC and 1450BC.

The queen's bathroom

Light entered the building through shafts

Experts think that over 30,000 people lived in the palace and surrounding area.

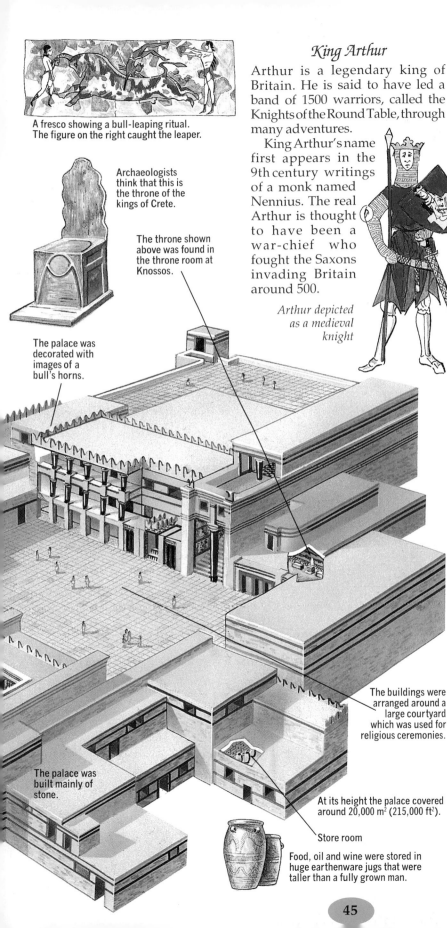

A fresco showing a bull-leaping ritual. The figure on the right caught the leaper.

Archaeologists think that this is the throne of the kings of Crete.

The throne shown above was found in the throne room at Knossos.

The palace was decorated with images of a bull's horns.

The palace was built mainly of stone.

The buildings were arranged around a large courtyard which was used for religious ceremonies.

At its height the palace covered around 20,000 m² (215,000 ft²).

Store room

Food, oil and wine were stored in huge earthenware jugs that were taller than a fully grown man.

King Arthur

Arthur is a legendary king of Britain. He is said to have led a band of 1500 warriors, called the Knights of the Round Table, through many adventures.

King Arthur's name first appears in the 9th century writings of a monk named Nennius. The real Arthur is thought to have been a war-chief who fought the Saxons invading Britain around 500.

Arthur depicted as a medieval knight

Arthur presiding over his court, with his knights gathered at a round table

In the 12th century, monks at Glastonbury Abbey claimed to have uncovered the bodies of Arthur and his wife, Guinevere. It is uncertain whether they really did find the bones, or whether they hoped to raise money from pilgrims attracted by the find.

The elusive priest-king

The legend of Prester John began as early as the 12th century among Crusaders (see page 23). He was said to be a wealthy Christian priest-king who lived in the East.

In the 15th and 16th centuries people believed Prester John lived in Abyssinia (now Ethiopia). Many adventurers set off to find him, including Pedro da Covilhã, from the Portuguese court. Prester John was never found, but stories of him persisted into the 16th century.

An illustration of Prester John from a book of 1540

Fact or fiction?

The Golden mask. In 1876 Heinrich Schliemann excavated the city of Mycenae in Greece and found a body wearing a gold mask. He thought it was the face of King Agamemnon, a hero of Greek myths, but the mask belonged to a much earlier king.

The mask found by Schliemann

c.2649-2150BC Period of Old Kingdom in Egypt.

2262-2162BC Life of Pepi II, King of Egypt who reigned for 94 years.

c.2550BC The reign of Khufu of Egypt, buried in Egypt's largest pyramid.

17th-11th century BC The Sang Dynasty rules China.

16th century BC Queen Ahhotep acts as regent for her son.

1504-1450BC The life of Tuthmosis III of Egypt, a warrior king.

1503BC Queen Hatshepsut becomes regent for her stepson, Tuthmosis III.

c.1411-1375BC The life of Amenhotep III of Egypt, who befriends his chief minister.

14th century BC Akhenaten becomes Pharaoh of Egypt, and worships Aten the Sun god.

1361-1352BC The reign of Tutankhamun of Egypt, whose grave was uncovered in 1922.

1304-1237BC Reign of Ramesses II of Egypt, a great builder.

1198-1167BC The reign of Ramesses III of Egypt, who suffers conspiracies at court.

7th century BC Amanirenas, queen mother of the Kingdom of Meroë in Africa, attacks Roman garrisons in southern Egypt.

5th century BC Queen Artemisia of Harlicarnassus fights at sea in Greece.

630-562BC The reign of Nebuchadnezzar II, who rebuilds the city of Babylon.

356-323BC The life of Alexander the Great, King of Macedonia.

353BC Death of King Mausolus of Halicarnassus, who is buried in a great tomb.

273BC Asoka, King of the Mauryan empire in India, leads his army to war. Appalled by the slaughter, he becomes a Buddhist.

259-210BC The life of Zheng, who takes the title First Emperor of China.

69-30BC The life of Cleopatra of Egypt, who marries a Roman general called Antony.

37-4BC The reign of Herod the Great, King of Judea, who builds five palaces, including Masada.

1st century Queen Boudicca leads a rebellion against Roman forces in England.

14-37 The reign of Tiberius, Emperor of Rome, whose close friend is a man named Sejanus.

37-41 The reign of Caligula, Emperor of Rome, who suffered periods of madness.

51-54 The reign of Claudius, Emperor of Rome, who is poisoned by his wife.

54-68 The reign of Nero, Emperor of Rome, who is said to have set fire to Rome.

267 Queen Zenobia rules the city of Palmyra and fights the Romans.

361 Julian becomes Emperor of Rome and worships Roman gods.

c.406-453 The life of Attila, King of an Asian tribe called the Huns.

c.500 A war-chief named Arthur fights the Saxons invading Britain.

584 King Chilperic of Neustria (now part of France) is murdered by his second wife Fredegond.

690 Wu Ze Tian seizes power and rules China.

751-68 The reign of Pepin the Short, King of the Franks.

771-814 The reign of Charlemagne, King of the Franks, a great patron of the arts.

c.956-1015 The life of Vladimir, ruler of the kingdom of Kiev.

987-996 The reign of Hugh Capet, King of France who replaces the Carolingian kings previously in power.

c.995-1030 The life of King Olaf Haraldsson of Norway, a Christian king. On one of his raids, Olaf pulls down London Bridge with grappling irons.

1066 William, Duke of Normandy, conquers England and becomes king.

1102-67 The life of Matilda, who, despite her efforts, is never crowned Queen of England.

1118-70 The life of Thomas Becket, Archbishop of Canterbury, close friend of Henry II of England and later a saint.

1216-72 The reign of Henry III of England, who becomes king at the age of nine.

1226 Blanche of Castille becomes regent for Louis IX of France.

1226-70 The reign of Louis IX of France, who joined the Crusades.

1272-1307 The reign of Edward I of England who marries Eleanor of Castille.

1306 The coronation of Robert I (1274-1329) of Scotland, known as Robert Bruce.

1359 Dom Pedro (1334-69), son of Alfonso XI of Portugal, marries Inez de Castro.

1362 A merchant called Giovanni is told by his dying mother that he is John I, rightful King of France.

1380-1422 Reign of Charles VI of France, who suffers from periods of madness.

1394-1460 The life of Prince Henry the Navigator, a Portuguese patron of explorers.

15th century The brutality of the prince of Wallachia (in modern Romania) gains him the name "Vlad the Impaler".

1413-22 The reign of Henry V of England, who invades France and wins the Battle of Agincourt.

1466-1519 The life of Montezuma, the last Aztec Emperor of Mexico.

1483 The reign of Edward V of England, one of the princes imprisoned in the Tower of London.

1485-1509 The reign of Henry VII of England, whose throne is claimed by two pretenders, Lambert Simnel and Perkin Warbeck.

1494-1566 The life of Süleyman the Magnificent, Sultan of Turkey, who marries a woman named Roxelana.

1509-47 The reign of Henry VIII of England, who marries six times.

1533 The largest ransom ever is paid for the life of Atahualpa, King of Peru.

1533 Henri, future Henri II of France, marries Catherine de Medici, but he is in love with Diane de Poitièrs, his mistress.

1530-84 The reign of Ivan IV, Tsar of Russia, known as Ivan the Terrible.

1533-84 The life of Prince William of Orange, killed by an assassin.

1542-87 The life of Mary, Queen of Scots, who marries her cousin Lord Darnley.

1542-1605 The life of Akbar the Great, one of the greatest Mogul emperors.

1558-1603 The reign of Elizabeth I of England, patron of the arts.

1566-1603 Life of Mahomet III, an Ottoman Sultan, who kills his brothers to ensure his throne.

1566-1625 The life of James I of England, who also rules Scotland.

1580-1663 The life of Jinga Mbandi, Queen of Matamba, West Africa, who gains independence for her kingdom.

1590-1617 The life of Sultan Ahmet I of Turkey, who introduces the Cage.

1592-1666 The life of Shah Jahan, one of the most powerful emperors of India.

1603 The False Dimitri invades Russia and is crowned tsar.

1617-82 The life of Lobsang Gyatso, the fifth ruler of Tibet, known as the Dalai Lama.

1625-49 The reign of Charles I, the only English king to be executed.

1638-1715 The life of Louis XIV of France, for whom the Palace of Versailles is built.

1660-85 The reign of Charles II of England, during which Colonel Blood attempts to steal the English crown jewels.

1665-1714 The life of Anne, Queen of England.

1682-1721 The reign of Peter the Great, Tsar of Russia, who builds the city of St. Petersburg.

1693-1740 The life of Anna of Russia, who treats her courtiers harshly.

1712-86 The life of Frederick the Great, King of Prussia, a formidable military leader.

1715-74 The reign of Louis XV of France, whose mistress is Madame de Pompadour.

1745 Bonnie Prince Charlie invades England, claiming the throne as the grandson of James II.

1746-1803 The life of Toussaint L'Ouverture, a revolutionary leader of the black slaves on the island of Haiti, in the Caribbean.

1760-1820 The reign of George III of England, who suffers from periods of madness.

1762-96 The reign of Catherine of Russia, known as "the Great".

1762-1830 The life of George IV of England, who builds the Royal Pavilion at Brighton and marries Caroline of Brunswick.

1774-93 The reign of Louis XVI of France, who dies with his wife Marie Antoinette at the guillotine.

1787-1828 The life of warrior Shaka, leader of the Zulu kingdom.

1804-15 The reign of Napoleon Bonaparte, First Consul and Emperor of France.

1810 The Duke of Cumberland, son of George III of England, is attacked by his valet.

1837-1901 The reign of Victoria, Queen of England.

1845-86 The life of Ludwig II of Bavaria, whose great passions are building and the music of a composer named Wagner.

1857 Lakshimbai, the Rani of the Kingdom of Jhansi, joins rebel leaders in a revolt against the British occupying India.

c.1871-1916 The life of Rasputin, friend and adviser to Tsar Nicholas II of Russia.

1889 Prince Rudolph, heir to the Austro-Hungarian Empire, is discovered dead at Mayerling.

1893-1976 The life of Mao Tse-tung, a Chinese leader.

1901-89 The life of Emperor Hirohito of Japan, who lives as god-king until 1946.

1918 Tsar Nicholas II of Russia is shot with his family at Yekaterinburg.

1920 Anna Anderson claims to be Anastasia, daughter of Tsar Nicholas II of Russia.

1924 Pu Yi, the last Chinese Emperor, leaves the Forbidden City.

1937 Edward VIII of England gives up his throne to marry Mrs Simpson, a divorcee.

1953 The coronation of Elizabeth II of Great Britain and Northern Ireland.

1959 Tenzin Gyatso, the 14th Dalai Lama of Tibet, flees to India.

1963 John F. Kennedy, President of the United States, is assassinated in Dallas, Texas.

1974 The coronation of Jigme Singe Wangchuck of Bhutan.

1975 King Juan Carlos is restored to the Spanish throne.

Index

The publisher would like to thank the following organizations for permission to reproduce their material: The Ancient Art and Architecture Collection, cover, 7, 18, 35; The Bridgeman Art Library, London, 30, 34; Express Newspapers plc, 43; The Hulton Deutsch Collection, London, 1, 10, 21, 29, 40; The Mansell Collection, London, 19, 33; The Office of Tibet, London, 10; Popperfoto, 27, 31, 37; Press Association, 43; Range Pictures Ltd, 42; The Royal Collection © Her Majesty Queen Elizabeth II, 43; Saudi Arabia Information Centre, 43; Times Books, 40

First published in 1995 by Usborne Publishing Ltd, Usborne House, 83-85 Saffron Hill London EC1N 8RT, England.
Copyright © 1995 Usborne Publishing Ltd. The name Usborne and the device ⚇ are Trade Marks of Usborne Publishing Ltd.
UE. First published in America in August 1995
Printed in Spain

Governor's Reading Initiative 1998